PRAISE FO

SPEAKING WITH STRATEGIC IMPACT

"I'm a big fan of Kate's training and coaching—both for myself and for our people. Her approach is part of our executive development and her vocabulary is deeply embedded in our culture. If you don't want to just *talk the talk*, but *walk the walk* too—read this book!"

—LAURA THOMPSON
Executive Vice President & Chief Financial Officer,
The Goodyear Tire & Rubber Company

"After participating in Kate's training, it's not unusual for even a very experienced executive to walk up to me and say: 'I just learned a whole lot more than I expected.' I have little doubt that readers of this book will have the same reaction."

—JIM WOODRUM
Clinical Professor of Executive Education,
Northwestern University: Kellogg School of Management

"Kate taught me the value of preparation. I get a lot of compliments about my comfort on the stage, and that's 100% related to my level of preparation. I prepare enough to make it look like I 'wing it,' but the reality is that I do anything but. I've used Kate's techniques in every large speech I've given since the time I took her class, and it all starts with preparation and knowing your audience. Both my firm and I have definitely benefitted from Kate's class."

—RENAE T. FLANDERS, CPA
Chief Financial Officer,
Aon Risk Solutions, U.S. Retail

"Kate LeVan positions you for success! This book lays out her well-honed and proven strategy for creating and delivering a compelling and engaging presentation. We're proud to have worked with Kate for over ten years."

—JON BUTCHER
CEO, Mintel Americas, Mintel Group Ltd.

"For years, as SVP of HR, I saw firsthand the impact Kate could have on executive presentation skills with my colleagues in the C-suite. Since those days, Kate has been my exclusive recommendation for any executive wishing to elevate their presentation skills. Now I will be recommending they read her book as well."

—STEVE KING
Executive Director of the Center for Professional and Executive Development,
Wisconsin School of Business

"I highly recommend Kate's methods to transform your presentation skills. It was the fuel that got me the last mile on my journey to the executive level."

—ED McGROGAN
Senior Vice President and Chief Accounting Officer,
Discover Financial Services

"I cannot overemphasize the impact that the communication process Kate describes in this book had on my career over the last 20 years. As I used her tools with fanatical discipline (I took Kate's 2-day course many times), I began to become more efficient—able to do meaningful preparation even when only given 10–15 minutes to prepare. I was a finance guy by trade, but became a good communicator by reputation.

"This book will certainly impact the way you think about communication. The challenge is not only to let it impact the way you *think*, but also to embrace it, practice it, and use it with your team so it changes the way you *execute* communication— every time."

—DARREN WELLS
*former Executive Vice President, CFO and President, Europe,
The Goodyear Tire & Rubber Company [retired]*

"Kate's coaching helped me personally take that big next step in progressing my career and personal impact—I think the book provides great insight and direction to help you adapt and improve your ability to understand your audience and ensure you are able to connect effectively across the spectrum of executive styles you encounter. A great read for all consultants!"

—GARY FINK
Senior Managing Director, Global Consultancy

SPEAKING
WITH
STRATEGIC
IMPACT

*Wishing you
great success!
Kate LiSur
2018*

SPEAKING
=== WITH ===
STRATEGIC IMPACT

*Four Steps to Extraordinary
Presence & Persuasion*

Master the presentation discipline favored by
top corporations and business schools

KATE LEVAN

DP
DELTON PRESS
EVANSTON, ILLINOIS

Published by Delton Press
Evanston, Illinois

Cover and Interior Design by Imagine! Studios
www.ArtsImagine.com

Cover Photo: iStock.com/Rawpixel

ISBN: 978-0-9989759-0-0 (paperback)
ISBN: 978-0-9989759-1-7 (e-book)

Library of Congress Control Number: 2017907534

First Delton Press printing: May 2017

CONTENTS

OVERVIEW: THE PROCESS & ITS IMPLICATIONS 1
Avoid procrastination. Be strategic instead.

STEP ONE: THE WHO 17
Don't ignore the elephant in the room

STEP TWO: THE WHAT 33
Decide what you want them to think and feel—not just do

STEP THREE: THE WAY. 49
Map out your storyline first

STEP FOUR: THE HOW 75
You should be their most important visual (and aural) aid

TAKING THE MEASURE OF YOUR SUCCESS . . 129
Optional, but highly recommended

INTRODUCTION

Is this book for you?

Many fine books have been written about one of the most common of human fears—public speaking. This is not another one of those books.

If it were, I'd be violating my first rule of effective communication: make it about the audience. When we focus on our own fears—combating or compensating for them—we make it about ourselves. A presentation then becomes a matter of living through a self-centered ordeal, instead of a means of accomplishing real objectives like connecting with an audience, sharing our insights and gaining agreement. Although I empathize, my focus here is not on the deeply fear-stricken. If you count yourself among them, all I can offer is the sense of control and freedom from anxiety that comes as a happy by-product of the practices outlined in this book.

Nevertheless, the fear of public speaking does make for robust book sales. Google the phrase and you get more than

4,000,000 results. But my years of consulting and coaching experience suggest a more moderate, if chronic, affliction in the business arena. If you're like most of the diverse professionals I train and coach in face-to-face effectiveness, you're typically a high-functioning type who manages to make it through most presentations and usually gets invited back, despite minor bouts of anxiety and the occasional testing of an audience's patience.

You're experienced. Your job requires you to speak at least occasionally before a group of peers, external clients or senior management. You may even have had some type of training, or at least have "seen it done" by other colleagues in the field. You know enough to stand and speak up in front of large audiences; use slides everyone can see; sit down in a more casual meeting; include some sort of agenda; look around the room when you speak and try to avoid fidgeting and too many fillers (if you're conscious of them). You may even be adept at throwing in a story or two.

More than anything else, though, you dread the chaos around preparing for a new presentation and, if given a choice, will recycle old slides or just wing it. Your nervousness is often limited to those first few moments when you hear your own voice and before you somehow establish a connection with your audience—after which you rather courageously plow ahead with your audience in tow. More often than not, you do a respectable job that suits the modest expectations of the average business audience. You carry on because you trust that your presentations will make a difference—for your clients, your company and you.

If this profile generally fits, then this book is for you.

It's written for all those who tend to make their living—or their mark—through presentations long and short—the consultants, the analysts, the pitch team, the roadshow executives, the technology specialists, the project managers, the internal and external marketers, the sales reps and those subject matter experts (bless their hearts) who get dragged along with them on client calls. Bravo! You must be doing something right to be put in front of customers and decision-makers time and again.

But is it enough? Do you have enough to show for all the time you spend preparing for and delivering those presentations? Do you find that you and your team sometimes are "presenting" more than actually achieving your goals, furthering projects, increasing your win rate or getting credit for the assist? Is it possible that you squander precious opportunities in front of decision-makers or conference audiences by being adequate versus exceptional and compelling? Is there something more you could be doing?

Okay, those are the high-minded, doubt-raising questions. Of course, as a professional you're always looking for ways to do things better and more efficiently. But allow me to sharpen the picture of opportunity for you.

Look at it this way:

In a field where a presentation's content is often based on a questionable formula of how many slides can be read in the time allotted, where being able to "wing it" becomes the developmental goal, and the measure of success is whether or not you got through all your slides, there are ample opportunities to be *absolutely extraordinary.*

Simply exceed your audience's average expectations by giving them an engaging and productive experience *as a matter of deliberate practice.* This makes you an *extraordinary* presenter. And exceptionally good things tend to come to extraordinary presenters in our business culture—things like winning, increased sales, more exposure, more senior-level contacts, more responsibility, more . . . well, you get the idea.

This book focuses only on the presentation and communication practices that will help you be *consistently extraordinary* in the eyes of your audiences, with all the good outcomes that may mean for you. Think of it as an accelerated how-to to take you, in the words of Jim Collins, from "good to great" as a presenter.*

> *Exceed your audience's average expectations by giving them an engaging and productive experience* **as a matter of deliberate practice.**

Most of my training and coaching clients aren't lacking in experience. What they may lack are things such as a deep enough intelligence about their audience, or a communication objective that is appropriately persuasive and scaled to the situation at hand. They may lack clarity and structure to their key messages or a delivery style that is congruent with their purpose. They may be long on strategy and

---

* *Good to Great: Why Some Companies Make the Leap and Others Don't,* by James C. Collins, HarperCollins Publishers, October 16, 2001.

insight, but short on empathy and impact. Or, they're all about technique and impact, but perhaps seem inauthentic and less substantive.

So, the question becomes, how does the ordinary presenter bring it all together to achieve what is *extraordinary?* That's where you and your team may need *better practices* around presentations as well as some practical coaching advice. You've already got the hard-won experiences and probably a lot of intuitive observations that you just may not be leveraging right now. Are you ready to take it to the next level?

The following chapters outline an approach and offer specific strategic and tactical advice to keep you more consistently on the mark in your presentations. They represent a compilation of the advice that my training and coaching clients have told me has been most helpful and *differentiating* for them.

I recommend that you read the chapters in order, to keep the strategic considerations ahead of the tactical. Once you know how to implement the overall approach and why it's to your advantage to do it this way, you can then focus on the aspects needed to balance your own presentation practice and enjoy more consistent success.

By the way, I also highly recommend that you share these practices with 1) those who assist you in creating presentations—to give you proper support and keep you honest; *and* 2) those with whom you co-present—to keep things sane in the planning meetings and rehearsals.

Presenting—like all communication—is a skill, a means to an end. It can be practiced and perfected. Allow me to offer a key to mastering the means by which you make a living and a difference in the world.

Go forth and be extraordinary!

Kate LeVan
Evanston, Illinois
May 2017

THE PROCESS & ITS IMPLICATIONS

Avoid procrastination.
Be strategic instead.

THERE'S OFTEN A sinking feeling that emerges after you learn you have an opportunity to address an audience. Even for the experienced presenter, the first flush of anticipation can give way to a frantic chain of questions and what-ifs:

- What are their expectations?
- How do I set up the topic or issue?
- How can I engage the audience?
- Do I have enough time to prepare?
- What if they don't buy what I say?
- Do I have enough to say to fill the time?

▶ Will there be questions?

▶ What if there aren't any questions?

▶ How many slides should I use? Etc., etc., etc.

This undercurrent of bothersome questions is commonly addressed with procrastination. As an experienced presenter, you may use procrastination as your self-justified recourse, simply because you've "pulled something together" many times before or have had to "pull it off" in the end more than once. With so many questions to address, it seems easier to delay action until something has to happen or time just runs out. This leaves you with the last-minute choice of two presenting behaviors that can result in the mediocre, hit-or-miss performances we see in the vast majority of business presentations: *data dumping* or *winging it*.

DO YOU DATA DUMP OR WING IT?

Data dumping is the last resort of choice for most presenters. It seems a good strategy to cover all the bases first as preparation and then just talk about the slides during the actual presentation. Data dumpers compile every slide they could possibly use with the reasoning that they'll edit during the presentation based on the audience's response. Sometimes a formula of X number of slides per minute is used to make sure the time is filled adequately. Any rehearsal that occurs becomes a matter of ensuring they can make the slides "hang together."

Unfortunately, when you start with the slides, more often than not you will be driven by the slides. You can tell this is happening when the words "on this slide you can see" or "on the next slide" is used for every transition throughout the presentation. This is mind-numbing for the audience. And, when the focus is on making the slides "hang together," there's less chance that there will be any real focus on the audience and their reaction to the slides. This is when an audience can experience a presentation as data dumping, and the only salvation for the speaker is when someone in the audience takes control and interrupts the one-way flow of information with a question that focuses the discussion. This provides direction for a period of time and often obviates the need for many of the subsequent slides.

Unfortunately, when you start with the slides, more often than not you will be driven by the slides.

However, the detour taken may or may not be consistent with the presenter's sense of completeness. That's why those prone to data dumping often feel the need to drag their audiences through the very last slide anyway.

In these situations, the speaker is forgetting that a successful presentation has little to do with covering bases or getting through all the slides. Rather, it has everything to do with whether you gave the audience what *they* needed to help you achieve your objective with them. This objective, and your relationship with the audience, should have been thought about long before any slides were compiled in the first place.

The second last-minute coping behavior is "winging it." The tendency here is to put the anxiety around all those unanswered questions on hold until you're in front of your audience. Preparation just involves a simple decision to bring along the existing set of slides. It's the flip side of the same procrastination behavior. Generally, it makes for a peaceful night's sleep . . . until those moments right before the presentation, when you're chatting with a few of the folks who will be in the audience and perhaps gain clues to their expectations, their prejudices and their real knowledge base. Or even worse, you're already up there, and you begin wondering about these things and editing your thoughts—even while you're speaking! I've had some clients who can't even clearly recall what they said. (This is an out-of-body experience often confused with being able to think on your feet—except there isn't any presence of mind, much less "Presence" in the rhetorical sense. More on this in **Step Four: The How.**)

Many die-hard wingers insist that the nature of their particular job or role is to blame for their propensity to just start talking. I recently spoke to the CFO of a financial services firm who gave this excuse for his folks: "My analysts are usually answering questions from investors in a conference setting, so they don't have time to prepare. Maybe we should focus more on their delivery technique, so they don't talk on and on so much and use all those fillers."

Chances are, if they researched ahead of time who they were talking to, or paused and asked a clarifying question, they would know where they were going and wouldn't babble and use filler words. Pausing as a technique to avoid fillers is a good habit. Having a strategic goal to your answer is better. Actually, in the average business presentation or Q&A session, it can be extraordinary!

Of course, it doesn't always turn out badly. There's a chance that you, data dumper or winger, could learn some critical information at the last minute and successfully adapt your presentation on the fly. But why leave it to chance? Why keep subjecting yourself to the angst in the first place? It's tantamount to saying that haphazard results are good enough.

WHAT IT MEANS TO BE STRATEGIC IN A PRESENTATION

I'm suggesting that you be more strategic and take the lesson from such positive turnaround situations. The lesson is the following:

When things do go well, the turning point usually comes when you learn something about the audience and you're in a position to do something about it. You're not playing an anxious guessing game anymore. You know their expectations, and you have the information and resources at hand to fulfill them or manage them confidently.

This means that if you want to be a more strategic presenter, you need to make it your first order of business to Know Thy Audience—to whatever degree humanly possible before you begin.

For all you marketing types out there, all I'm doing is taking a page from Marketing 101 and applying it to interpersonal communication.

What do companies do when they want to launch a new product or service? They immerse themselves in their target audience. They interview them, they get third party research on them, they develop a composite profile of them, they test market their ideas and get their audience's feedback. And they do all this *before* they formally present their product or service to them. It's a proven approach that can work for you as a presenter, too. The trick is to make it your default mechanism in whatever time you have before you present.

> *If you want to be a more strategic presenter, you need to make it your first order of business to Know Thy Audience— to whatever degree humanly possible before you begin.*

BEWARE OF "PERFORMANCE MODE"

You see, it's human nature to default to making the presentation event about *you*. This causes us to go into "performance mode," when we focus more on how we will be viewed and rated by an audience versus focusing on having an authentic exchange of energy and ideas with that audience. Just think about some of those plaguing questions again:

▶ What are their expectations (**of me**)?
▶ Where do **I** start?

▶ What do **I** say?

▶ Do **I** have time?

▶ Will there be questions **(I can't answer)**?

▶ What if there aren't questions **(and I feel naked up there!)**?

This ego stuff is also the source of the procrastination, word-for-word memorization and, yes, fear. So, when you feel these coming on, instead of pulling out your hair, pulling out the old slides or deciding to wing it, you should default to a critical path to presentation success that begins with *the Who, not you!*

This critical path involves a four-step planning process that keeps the audience front and center in your consideration:

▶ Step One: The Who
▶ Step Two: The What
▶ Step Three: The Way
▶ Step Four: The How

If you remember these four simple steps—and execute them in this order—you'll be well on your way to more consistent success in your presentations. What follows is a quick explanation of the process as a whole and a suggestion for how to use it as a project-planning tool. Subsequent chapters will be devoted to amplifying the details of each step and giving you more insights, examples and tips to assist you in becoming an extraordinary presenter.

THE FOUR-STEP CRITICAL PATH AND ITS BENEFITS

▶ **Step One: The Who.** This step is the key to overcoming your procrastination, because now you know where to start—by getting the real target in sight. Once you learn you have a presentation to deliver and know its general topic and purpose, jump right on it by first analyzing your audience. It's the strategic place to start. In whatever time you have, find out everything you reasonably can about *who* your audience is—and what they think and feel about you, the situation, and your topic. If you can, get others to help you. Be creative. Ask questions and listen deeply. The more you learn about who and what you're dealing with, the calmer you'll get. The answers to the niggling questions that begin with "what, how or what if?" will emerge from here and be resolved much faster. More than any other step, this is where you can outdo any competition. The chapter on this step is about paying attention to the things that can make the biggest difference.

▶ **Step Two: The What.** There are two questions to address in this step: A) What is your real and immediate objective? and B) What key messages/evidence will support that objective? Once you have a working sense of who you're trying to influence or persuade, get crystal clear about your objective for them. This is the lynchpin of the entire process. What do you want these folks to

PLANNING PROCESS

Use these Four Steps as a project planner for all your presentations to keep them strategically on target.

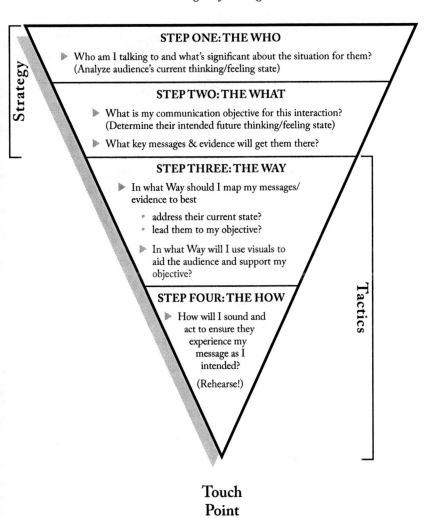

STEP ONE: THE WHO

▶ Who am I talking to and what's significant about the situation for them? (Analyze audience's current thinking/feeling state)

STEP TWO: THE WHAT

▶ What is my communication objective for this interaction? (Determine their intended future thinking/feeling state)

▶ What key messages & evidence will get them there?

STEP THREE: THE WAY

▶ In what Way should I map my messages/ evidence to best

    * address their current state?
    * lead them to my objective?

▶ In what Way will I use visuals to aid the audience and support my objective?

STEP FOUR: THE HOW

▶ How will I sound and act to ensure they experience my message as I intended?

(Rehearse!)

Strategy

Tactics

Touch
Point

think, to feel, to do as a result of your presentation? State it to yourself clearly and succinctly early on; because if *you* can't, there's little chance the audience will be able to grasp your point despite an hour of listening to you talk. Then brainstorm around the most compelling data, examples, stories, analogies, pictures or even gimmicks that you can use to get them to where you want them to be both intellectually *and* emotionally. The corresponding chapter on this step will help you formulate more persuasive and actionable presentation objectives.

▶ **Step Three: The Way.** Now you've got most of the pieces, and it's time to decide on order and structure, i.e., *the way* you will lead your audience to their enlightenment. But hold on—don't give in to that inclination to fire up the PowerPoint just yet! Like any good author or actor, you need to consider the total effect you're going for—you need to map your storyline and the flow of information first. The good news is that there's a tried and true way to do this that not only will keep you on target, but will also help your audience easily take in your message—and more likely remember it, too. Once this map is laid out, only then is it time to decide whether a few key slides or some other type of visual aid might be helpful in supporting or highlighting your key messages. To learn the three most common structural mistakes made by presenters and how to avoid them, don't skip reading more about this step.

▶ **Step Four: The How.** Now it's time for the *pièce de résistance*—and here I am speaking more about actual resistance. This is where even the most experienced presenters often fall short of their goal: rehearsal. That's because they spend precious time endlessly tweaking their slides instead of attending to the "icing on the cake" or what their audience will actually see and hear.

The fact is, more than half of the overall impact of your presentation is in *how* the audience members visually, aurally and tactically experience it.* Don't leave this to chance! Years of coaching have taught me that something always changes in rehearsal. And, if you don't know what that might be, why risk it in front of the audience? A translation must take place from the written word to performance art. It's the difference between reading a play and seeing it come alive on stage. For some differentiating rehearsal and delivery tips, consult this chapter.

That's the process. Now you just have to make it a discipline. Think of the four steps as a project-planning template next time you have a presentation to prepare. Get out your calendar and work backward from the date/time of the presentation to slot in everything from your audience analysis (the Who) to rehearsal time (the How). Being this explicit is especially important if you're presenting with someone else. For

---

* This is a safe estimate. Despite all the recent qualifications of Prof. Albert Mehrabian's famous research on feeling and attitudinal content, a review of more current research cited by the The Nonverbal Group (nonverbalgroup.com) estimates that nonverbal content can weigh in anywhere from 60%–90%, depending on the situation and individual.

example, let's say you have a conference presentation coming up next week.

Thursday: Noon/lunch—Meet with Sam for strategy session
  Goal: Analyze audience & agree on objective—capture key ideas &
  discuss respective roles (Steps 1&2)
Friday: Call conference planner to answer outstanding questions
  about audience/test ideas; finalize strategy with Sam/separately
  map out our presentations (Steps 1&3)
Monday/Tuesday: Visual Aids info pulled/created (Step 3)
Tuesday p.m.: Talk through slides with Sam; finalize flow (Step 3)
Wednesday: Individual rehearsals/editing as needed (Steps 3&4)
Thursday: Conf. room B—
  Walk through w/Sam at 4:00 p.m. (Step 4)
Friday a.m.: Conf. room B—
  Final dress rehearsal w/Sam (Step 4)
Friday: Showtime! Meet in lobby @ Hilton 12:45 p.m.;
  Equipment check 1 p.m.; presentation 2 p.m.
Friday p.m.: Drinks and debrief (review Steps 1-4)

Admittedly, there will be situations where you have much less time than this and must telescope the process. It may not be optimal, but it's also not an excuse to throw out what works. It's during these situations—when the VP's assistant is leaving multiple messages asking for slides that don't yet exist—that sticking to even an abbreviated version of the process will keep you sane. You'll have to go the extra mile in those situations anyway, so you might as well spend your precious time wisely and work smart to ensure a successful outcome. Believe me, the audience (if not the harried assistants) will appreciate it too. Here's why.

By following this approach, you'll probably have fewer slides—something rare and wonderful in most audiences' experience. We all know there's usually an inverse relationship between the number of slides a speaker has and the dynamism of the presentation. You will also be more *engaging* because you're putting the audience—what they know, feel and need—first. And, there's nothing more interesting to an audience member than feeling attended to.

If you're like many people to whom I introduce this practice, you're comfortable with the logic of what I'm proposing, but may get uneasy about the idea of not having everything you say on a slide. Some say that their clients even require it.

We've all seen these presentations. The first slide has a subject title like "Presentation to XYZ Company" with the presenter's name proudly inscribed on it; the second slide is entitled "Background"; the third is a list of topics (intended for use as an agenda); and the rest represent everything we can possibly say about the topics in bullet point or graph format to make ourselves look smart. And there we have it! What's more, those who can't attend the presentation can read this as a printed handout and not have missed a thing! Are they truly *not missing anything in not meeting you?* Now there's a disturbing question!

This is *not* a presentation. And, really, wouldn't it be better if the rave reviews of your presentation compelled the no-shows to follow up with you personally?

PRESENTATION CORRECTLY DEFINED

I'm not proposing that you do anything career-limiting. If your audience assessment suggests that the client's sense of a worthwhile presentation means 40+ slides or they'll feel cheated—then give it to them. But let's not do it at the expense of devaluing *you* as their value-added consultant. Remember, you may have a larger objective to achieve. Whether you choose to spend precious time with a prospect going through every last slide has to do with strategic delivery considerations you can read more about in the chapter on **FAQs: Applying the four-step process.**

But there are a few things implicit in the practice I'm suggesting that we might as well clarify right here.

▶ A presentation is *an interactive event during which you deliver information persuasively to an audience*—with or without the support of visual aids. Even if you're doing most of the talking, there should be an intentional exchange of energy going on. So, your planning has to start by assessing the current state of energy in the room with the conscious determination of influencing it somehow. You need to view yourself as a causal agent.

▶ If you start your preparation by creating the slides, you're starting with the tactical considerations and are not being strategic in your presentation planning. Results will more likely be haphazard, depending on how the "energy" in the room responds.

▶ PowerPoint slides may be the most common and convenient type of visual aid, but not the only or necessarily the best visual aid.

▶ That set of slides is not your presentation.

▶ A "presentation" is not the same as a "leave behind document."

▶ *You* are the most essential visual aid. *You*, interacting with your slides (or other material), are the presentation.

Granted, these are not assumptions shared by the majority of corporate citizens. That's what makes them differentiating. It's also what can make the practice sometimes challenging to observe. So, start small—with the presentations you have control over. Make a splash. Get a following. Then, let the rest of them in on your secret!

One of my former clients observed this presentation practice within his treasury department as standard operating procedure. Team members routinely conferred on audience insights, objectives and strategy before important meetings. They mapped out their individual presentations and rehearsed in front of one another to test their approach. The department became renowned internally for their professionalism. Is it a coincidence that my client, the department head, was elevated to an officer of the company? I doubt the relationship was directly causal, but the discipline he exercised around his communication certainly helped.

There's no guarantee you'll become an officer of your company by following the four-step practice outlined above. But you'll at least have something proactive to do when that sinking feeling sets in the next time you need to prepare a presentation. More importantly, you can be confident that your approach will be more strategic and your tactical judgments the most sound.

THE WHO

Don't ignore the elephant in the room

A WEEK AFTER THE tragic events of 9/11/2001, I was scheduled to address a group of local business executives in Chicago on a timely topic—leadership communication. The prospect seemed daunting as I stood there about to begin. As you might expect, you could have cut the emotion in the room with a knife, and questions that I could never have anticipated just days before seemed sure to surface.

What was I going to *say* to these people? What *could* anyone say? We were physically removed from the epicenter of those terrible days, but psychically we weren't. Everyone seemed to have a story. One of my own colleagues had escaped from Tower Two of the World Trade Center. People were hurting all around us, and at the moment we couldn't do much of anything to make a difference. All this skill-building stuff just seemed so trivial. Clearly, something had to be said, but it couldn't be perfunctory.

Ultimately, I realized that I was not alone in my self-doubt and sense of awkwardness. So, that's where I began—sharing what I suspected was true for everyone in the room and commenting on the apparent triviality of it all. With riveted eyes and quiet nods, a bond was formed between us like so often happens in extreme situations. Gradually, with some time given over to sharing and acknowledging how overwhelmed we all felt, the relevance of what we were there to do—to stop being paralyzed and start leading—took hold. I had gained the tacit *emotional* permission I needed from my audience to continue, and I also gained tremendous insight into what they needed from me that evening.

To a great extent, decorum dictated that I acknowledge what was so obvious in the room that day. Any presenter would probably feel the need to do something similar. In fact, the magnitude of the disastrous

> *My point is this: we tend to mute our instincts in all but the most dramatic situations. In most business situations, speakers tend to overlook or consciously avoid the emotional atmosphere in which they're presenting.*

events of 9/11 forged a solidarity among my audience that probably made it easier for me to "read" and relate to them.

My point is this: we tend to mute our instincts in all but the most dramatic situations. In most business situations, speakers tend to overlook or consciously avoid the emotional atmosphere in which they're presenting.

THE *SINE QUA NON* OF A SUCCESSFUL PRESENTATION

The above story exemplifies the primacy of *connecting* with an audience before anything meaningful can happen. To do so, however, requires getting out of your own drama first and acknowledging what's going on emotionally for the other people in the room. In my situation, it was easy to discover something we had in common. This may not always be the case. But if you don't acknowledge the elephant in the room early on, you'll spend the rest of your time walking around it and not accomplishing all that much—or at least not as much as you could have.

I see this truth played out time and time again in my work with clients.

▶ A technology consultant fails to acknowledge huge differences in the experience levels of her audience members and how this might affect their interest level and the way they perceive her. She plays to the lowest common denominator and loses the decision-makers.

▶ A subject matter expert presents with the objective of getting a client to act on a proposal that's been languishing for months. He decides it would be too tension-filled (for him mostly) to refer directly to the proposal already on the table. The same ground is covered and no progress is made. (Little wonder that a typical day at work becomes a reenactment of the classic movie *Ground Hog Day!*)

▶ I'll hear lengthy background stories from a client about the favorable and unfavorable political dynamics within an audience to whom he will be presenting, and then watch as he plows ahead in his rehearsal with no apparent sensitivity to those dynamics.

In all these examples, something was emotionally at stake for the audience (or between presenter and audience) that either wasn't fully recognized, or was recognized, but not leveraged in a way that would have made a positive difference for all concerned.

If this is typical (and my exposure to countless business presentations says it is), there's a huge opportunity here to differentiate yourself by simply being aware that your audience is made up of human beings who are both rational *and* emotional. Once you can profile the audience's state(s) of mind more fully, you can then consciously choose to address commonalities, lay any differences on the line, beg pardon of the more experienced to brief the less experienced, etc. When you do these things, you will be forming an emotional connection with those audience members, the *sine qua non* of any successful presentation. Even in sensitive situations where agreement isn't expected, a productive disagreement at least requires an atmosphere of mutual respect and acknowledgment.

Any successful presentation begins with a set of working assumptions about what's going on—rationally and emotionally—for the people in the room and an honest assessment of your current relationship (or lack of relationship) with them. But how might this be different from what you're already doing now? My observation is that many presenters confuse their situation analysis with what I'm calling *audience analysis*. The following is an example of this and some tips to take into account when you're assessing *the Who* for your next presentation.

> *Any successful presentation begins with a set of working assumptions about what's going on— rationally and emotionally—for the people in the room and an honest assessment of your current relationship (or lack of relationship) with them.*

THINK AUDIENCE ANALYSIS, NOT SITUATION ANALYSIS

When I ask presenters to assess an audience, I typically hear something that sounds like this:

> *I'm not sure, but I think there will be about seventy-five to one hundred people there. My boss has asked me to brief regional field specialists on a new process being introduced in the third quarter of this year. They're real hands-on types who will be implementing the process at client locations. I'm told that a global management representative will also be sitting in on the session while he's in town—so we need to impress him. The new process is really revolutionary, and I want to get everyone excited about it! My concern is that I only have an hour. The process is a bit involved and I need to be engaging. So I was thinking about starting with a chart that shows . . .*

Here, the presenter has done a typical "situation analysis" and concluded that he has a tactical problem of fitting a lot of information into too short a time slot. So what's new? This is a classic example of where you will end up if you don't give adequate consideration to your audience.

The information provided tells us very little about what is true for this audience beyond some facts and observations about their numbers, their role and how the presenter needs to make them feel. There's even a hint of confusion about who the audience *really is* with the distraction of the "global management representative."

Unfortunately, my client in real life had already presented once on the basis of the above situation analysis with less than satisfactory results. Many of the field specialists resisted the new process and the global management rep wasn't impressed. When we deconstructed what happened after the fact as a learning opportunity, we came up with a very different kind of audience assessment that yielded a whole different approach for his next regional presentation.

The turning point came as a result of getting clear about who the primary audience was (the field specialists) and spending a little more time with what was *emotionally at stake* for them during that presentation. The elephant in the room was that this new process represented a major change for that audience. Change can induce things like fear, confusion and distrust of "exciting new initiatives" from corporate. Since they were more hands-on, a high-level briefing might be frustrating and anxiety-producing. In addition, many of them were not native English speakers (the presenter's only language).

Taking an audience from fear, confusion and distrust to enthusiastic adoption of a new process is no easy task, and it typically won't happen in one hour-long session. This realization was freeing for my client, who recast his next regional roadshow as a demonstration of the process with lots of time to answer questions and quell fears. A schedule of follow-up opportunities for feedback, training, and support was emphasized. He no longer viewed his task as a stand-alone presentation; it became part of a program of communication around the new process. Objections raised and addressed in one region paved the way for acceptance in the next. If management attended, they were briefed ahead of time about the overall buy-in strategy and the particular focus of that presentation. Needless to say, management was impressed.

AUDIENCE ANALYSIS THOUGHT-STARTERS

The lesson here is to go beyond the cursory checklist of who's going to be there, what their titles are, the purpose of the meeting and your own emotions about the experience. Instead, treat this as the investigative phase of your presentation planning, where questions rule. Stay with the questions as long as you reasonably can to uncover what is true for your audience.

> *Treat this as the investigative phase of your presentation planning, where questions rule. Stay with the questions as long as you reasonably can to uncover what is true for your audience.*

Ask yourself (or others) things like the following:

- ▶ What's going on for them?
- ▶ What's their current attitude toward me, toward the topic, toward others in the room?
- ▶ Is there anything they're expecting?
- ▶ What do they consider "a good meeting"?

▶ What are their objectives and how might they differ from mine?

▶ Who needs to be educated? Who needs to be persuaded? Do they want to be?

▶ If there's a decision to be made, how will they go about it?

▶ Who will influence whom in the group?

▶ Are there sensitive issues I need to address before we can proceed?

▶ Can I address these before the presentation?

▶ Will someone feel threatened by what I say?

▶ Is there something at risk for them in hiring or agreeing with me?

Answers to these types of questions will help you assess what can realistically be accomplished in that one presentation and help decide who and what to focus on. In sum, the decisions and working assumptions you come up with will guide your objective-setting and overall presentation strategy.

If you don't know the answers to these or other questions you deem critical, ask others close to the situation. You might even want to do a reality check on your own assumptions as well.

HOW TO GET—AND STAY— OUT OF YOUR HEAD

Here are some additional tips to keep you focused on *the Who*, instead of on *You*:

▶ Don't wait for the big meeting to create rapport with your audience. Ask the manager, client or prospect directly what they need and expect in advance to gain buy-in. My favorite question is some version of, *How can I make this meeting as productive as possible for you?*

▶ Beware of those who answer the above question with some variation of "Oh, just tell us a little bit about you and your services (or plans, or strategy, etc.)." They either haven't thought about the meeting or think they're being polite. More likely, they would prefer to hear about themselves and solutions to problems like their own. This is your opportunity to let them feel heard and help them prioritize.

▶ Don't forget to share your presentation strategy at the outset with your audience, because it could answer lingering questions they may have. For example, if your plan is to focus on one thing more than another, or if you are making certain assumptions, tell them why. Don't assume that everyone was filled in on conversations you had with individual audience members. If some in the room disagree, you're better off knowing this early on, when you still have a chance to bring them on board or can at least acknowledge their differing points of view.

▶ Don't assume that they read everything you sent them ahead of time, or remember the content if they did. But don't use this as an excuse to waste precious time (yours and theirs) recapping old stuff. In most situations, you'll want to quickly share your assumptions about what is known, ask them if they need further clarification, then move on to fulfill your objective.

▶ Consider your audience's communication style, or how they like to process information to come to a decision. Observe and listen to how they speak beforehand if you can, then translate what you hear into strategy. Are they all about the details and process? Then you should be the same in your presentation—logically lead them to a solid conclusion. Are they decisive? Give them the executive summary, and then let them feel smart by asking you a few confirming questions before declaring their decision. Are they prone to holding court and story-telling? Toss them an idea or situation and let them make it their own. These and other possible approaches are suggested in works by the highly-respected writer/researcher, Robert Bolton. They're worth a read.*

▶ If there's more than one point of view in the audience, then respectfully acknowledge this up front.

▶ If there's more than one elephant in the room, think about what you can do to gain consensus *before* the presentation and encourage cooperation.

▶ And finally, don't skip this first step if you "already know" a particular audience. Cover this base, albeit briefly, no

---

* See *Social Style/Management Style* by Robert and Dorothy Grover Bolton, et al., AMACOM, 1984.

matter what. Ask yourself if something has changed since you last saw them, or if there is something new at stake or at risk for them in the current situation.

ASSESSING EXTERNAL AUDIENCES WHEN THE STAKES ARE HIGH

I add the following tips for competitive pitch teams or when formally presenting to a large group unfamiliar to you.

▶ For conference presentations, call the most senior person you can to get information on what led them to pick your topic, the mix of conference attendees, some insight on what traditionally works and what doesn't in that forum, *plus the names of a few prominent attendees you can call and interview.* Ask those interviewed if you can reference the conversation in your presentation (i.e., "When I was talking to X, who so generously shared some pointed examples of this industry problem . . ."). There's no better way to make an industry conference feel almost intimate.

▶ Remember that the people who wrote the Request for Proposal are not necessarily the same people who are in the room making the decision about your presentation. The audience members you should be analyzing are the folks in the room, not the technical writers, marketing people, purchasing agent or conference coordinator.

▶ Spend *most* of your time on this *first* strategy step to get the whole team in sync on who they are trying to influence. Don't let the conversation devolve to worrisome questions about how much time you have to fill and what slides will be used.

▶ Include in this step plans for some intentionally orchestrated Q&A sessions with your prospect or client *before* the final presentation. This will build advance rapport with your evaluating audience and set expectations that your team not only wants the business, but is the frontrunner. What a great start to any pitch presentation!

▶ If you're working with a third-party consultant or purchasing agent who is organizing and conducting a search on behalf of the audience/prospect, you definitely want to make a friend. They could potentially be an influencer or champion of your cause. Go to great lengths to express respect for their process, but pose your issues, too. Go ahead and ask them questions like, How will you make this decision? What are your priorities? What would you like to accomplish, at minimum? Do you think everyone would say the same thing? Let them problem-solve around how to get you those answers, as it often leads to a bending of the rules. And, if they say they'll have to "share the answers with the other competing firms," say okay. You've already made it clear that you're smart and hungry for the business.

▶ If there's more than one communication style in the audience, defer to the decision-maker's style. If you don't know who that is, find out. If you can't, then use your best working assumptions. An audience of engineers may be process people, contract lawyers will get into details, sales people will tend to be bored by detail and want to know how to get more sales or commissions, amiable types will put a priority on everyone being heard and getting along. Test these assumptions and continue to learn about your audiences.

The best presenters have an ability to not only read, but also relate to an audience. They employ the proper content and tone needed to help the audience see or accept the value in what they have to offer. And, if there are any elephants in the room, they help their audience set these aside by telling them first "you've been heard." None of this is possible without a thorough analysis of your audience—both rationally and emotionally.

This first step of assessing, as best you can, the mindset of those who are actually in your audience is so critical that you'll want to

> *The best presenters have an ability to not only read, but also relate to an audience . . . And, if there are any elephants in the room, they help their audience set these aside by telling them first "you've been heard."*

consider it ongoing. (As any "winger" knows, you can always learn more about your audience right up to the actual presentation!) When you start *applying* this audience knowledge to the formulation of your objective and *making choices on the basis of your analysis* regarding persuasive evidence, presentation structure and delivery (see Steps Two–Four), *that's* when you know you're not only moving your audience toward your objective, but moving yourself—from simply being adequate to being more strategic and extraordinary.

THE WHAT

*Decide what you want them
to think and feel—
not just do*

N OW THAT YOU'VE assessed your audience and
have a set of working assumptions about what they
need rationally and emotionally, it's time to answer the following two questions: 1) What achievable objective can I have for
this presentation based on what I know about my audience?
and 2) What can I do, say and show to support that objective?

By the way, you may have to discipline yourself to address
them in this order.

I say this because I've noticed a curious thing about experienced presenters. Often, after painstakingly "reading" their
audience—their prejudices, lack of knowledge, political dynamics, or pure disinterest—they will default to doing exactly

what they've done before, as though the outcome will somehow be different this time or (worse) as though nothing they
say or do could ever make a difference! This usually indicates
a lack of clarity around one's own objective which is neither
strategic nor ultimately effective. If you can't articulate your
objective clearly, how can you expect the audience to get your
drift?

SCALING YOUR OBJECTIVE TO
THE REALITY IN THE ROOM

A more strategic approach involves scaling your objective
to what can reasonably be accomplished with that particular
audience in the course of one presentation and, then, seeing yourself as the causal agent who will create that "effect"
through what you do, say, and show. That's what effectiveness
is, after all.

Let's take an obvious example. Let's say your audience
members really are all ignorant with regard to your subject
matter or larger purpose. If your objective is "to be superior to
my audience" or "to create a mystique about what I do," then
go right ahead and tell them everything you know, regardless
of their ability to appreciate it. Of course, you won't be "connecting" with that audience; in fact, you may be creating just
the opposite effect.

More strategic objectives might be "to not threaten, but
to offer help," "to give them reason to question their assumptions," or "to give them an epiphany that will leave them
wanting more from me." These are examples of strategic objectives that are grounded in what you may know about the

rational or emotional needs of an audience. They reflect a realistic assessment of the presenter's relationship to the audience at the outset and propose a more incremental outcome as "successful." When you start planning from this type of objective, you'll be more likely to give them what *they* need and can handle in the moment—the key to effective communication.

This may seem like a remedial example, but it's critical. Too many presentations are delivered with the grand, generic (and usually unspoken) objectives of "making the sale" or "getting management's approval." These are objectives that are solely about the presenter and his/her goals and not necessarily about the audience members' needs given where they are in their decision-making process. These kinds of generic objectives are often at the root of meetings that go nowhere or, worse, meetings that get hijacked by the audience.

Obviously, you want the sale or management's Okay. The point is, what do *they* need in order to agree to give you that sale or their approval? It's important to make this distinction between *your* objective and that of the presentation. *Your* objective is likely the goal that got you in front of the audience in

> *Obviously, you want the sale or management's Okay. The point is, what do* they *need in order to agree to give you that sale or their approval? It's important to make this distinction between* your *objective and that of the presentation.*

the first place (e.g., *to gain senior management approval to create a new department for which I'll be the department head*). Your *presentation* objective has to do with the intentional outcome you have for the audience in that particular interaction (which should further your overall goal). It should have more to do with where *their* heads are at that stage of your discussion. This is where leveraging your audience analysis (the information you gained in **The Who** step) comes into play.

MOVING AN AUDIENCE FROM A CURRENT TO A FUTURE STATE

If you've done adequate audience analysis, you should have a sense of the audience's *current state* (i.e., what they are thinking, feeling, and doing or not doing vis-à-vis your proposal). In the last example, you might know person by person whether your proposal for a new department will be met with enthusiasm, doubt, or resistance and roughly why that is so. At this level, you probably have already done a lot of one-on-one consensus-building beforehand to get them to wherever they are right now. But between this in-depth audience analysis and the actual achievement of your business objective, there is the step of formulating your strategic communication objective for the next interaction. This is done by positing a *future state* for your audience (i.e., what they should reasonably be thinking, feeling, and doing as a result of your presentation). From here, you can derive a strategic and actionable objective that encapsulates your overall approach to that presentation and will serve to guide you in its preparation.

Let's say you know that the majority of senior managers view your proposal as a risk-worthy business venture, while the dissenters' issues are more cautionary yet surmountable. In this case, the *future state* to which you may want to move the audience would be one where all senior managers feel comfortable about the creation of a new department and its organizational implications. You may even detail what this implies, manager by manager (i.e., what each must know and/or feel to be generally in favor of your proposal). A summary strategic objective in this situation might be the following: *to ensure that the majority feel validated in their decision and the minority are reassured with the creation of a new corporate department and all the organizational changes this implies.* Such an objective would then be reflected in the presenter's tactical decision to balance an assumptive tone about the upcoming management decision with a collegial willingness to acknowledge or accommodate each manager's point of view as much as possible.

On the other hand, let's say your proposal has a good chance of going down in flames due to a clash of titan personalities. In this case, the desired future state for the audience might be one where there is a reasonable discussion around the pros and cons of your proposal that discourages rash dismissal by the naysayers and encourages giving it the old college try. Here, a more appropriate objective might be this: *to engage management in a strategic and structured discussion of the proposal, so that all feel good about having given it a "fair hearing" and are inclined to approve it on a "trial basis."* That's a very different kind of meeting and presentation. This objective would then drive the presenter's tactical approach to keep the proposal alive by adopting a certain style of presentation (more interactive and facilitative) and positioning the desired outcome as a trial to the management team.

The discipline around first describing in as much detail as possible (and probably more than I've outlined above) a "future state" for your audience members and then articulating a more distilled version of it that is your "strategic objective" may seem like a uselessly redundant exercise. Nevertheless, I have found that it better serves you as a presenter for several reasons.

OBJECTIVE-SETTING: THE LYNCHPIN OF THE PROCESS

First of all, this step forces you to go back to your audience analysis and deal with the realities of the dynamics in the room—both rational (e.g., the likely vote outcome) and emotional/attitudinal (e.g., how they will feel about the outcome and about you after all is said and done). It keeps you more accountable for addressing and managing, as much as possible, any of those elephants in the room. With a more detailed "future state" laid out before you, it's more difficult to blithely claim that your objective is "to get everyone in the room excited about the proposal." (I wish I had a dollar for every time I've heard *that* objective.)

Moreover, a full articulation of the future state to which you want to move your audience often holds the answers to many of the decisions you will need to make in preparing your presentation; such as, how to organize the meeting, its tone, opening remarks, what to emphasize, the type of persuasive evidence to use—even who to look at when you say something!

The ability to treat these as intentional choices is what makes this approach more "strategic," and your tactical preparation and delivery much more efficient.

> *A full articulation of the future state to which you want to move your audience often holds the answers to many of the decisions you will need to make in preparing your presentation.*

And, please don't abandon this process just because your presentation is at a conference in front of four hundred people you don't know. At least, not if you want to stand out as extraordinary. As noted in **Step One: The Who,** there are always questions to ask and people who can provide insight into the schools of thought represented in the audience. Reflecting such insights in your presentation will let the majority of listeners know they matter to you. Do the very best you can. It could mean the difference between a speaking invitation that serves as a pointless interruption to your business day and one that serves as a vehicle to more business!

In short, once the objective-setting process is complete, your stated objective will likely hold more meaning and imply more specific actions for you and your audience. All your decisions about the presentation thereafter can be tested against it. And, if you have co-presenters, it's an absolute godsend for keeping things on strategy.

So now what? We fire up the PowerPoint, right? Well, not just yet.

Better first to get all you'd like to get across out on the table. But don't start writing a script either. At this stage, you want to 1) brainstorm your key messages, 2) prioritize by combining and editing them based on how they fit with your objective, and then, 3) determine your most compelling evidence for the ones you will need to support or highlight.

Following are some additional insights to make this stage in your presentation planning as productive as possible.

BRAINSTORM RATIONAL *AND* EMOTIONAL KEY MESSAGES

List the key conversational points that you'd like to make to your audience as though you were talking to them—without all the angst associated with standing up in front of them and presenting. Jot down bullet point notes as they occur to you about the value your proposition has for them. Even better, speak them aloud as you go. It's here that you will discover a lot of headlines, phrasing and positioning that you can qualify (if necessary) later. The benefit of this approach comes from

> *Having thought through your strategic objective first, you are already being guided by this star, so the key messages you come up with will more likely be on the mark and useful.*

not restraining yourself—or your passion for your topic—with the requirement for something to flow perfectly. Besides, having thought through your strategic objective first, you are already being guided by this star, so the key messages you come up with will more likely be on the mark and useful. If not, just know that there will be later opportunities in the process to make needed adjustments. Note, also, that this brainstorm method has obvious advantages if you are crafting a joint presentation with multiple people.

Let me emphasize that you do still need to hold your audience's perspective here as best you can. This is no time to detach and go on a rant. Your messages will be effective only to the extent that they are persuasive to your audience and support your strategic objective. So, use your audience analysis to help you generate messages that appeal to both the rational and emotional sides of your audience. What will *they* get out of what you have to offer?

Messages that appeal to the *rational* benefits for the audience are what you'd expect in any business presentation. They answer questions such as: "How much money will your proposal (or process, initiative, idea, approach, etc.) make or save the organization?" and "How will it increase efficiency or productivity?" This is due diligence stuff when it comes to making a business case. Based on your audience analysis, you can probably already anticipate here what facts, statistics and comparisons will be the most compelling for which people.

But don't overlook *emotional* benefits in your listing of key messages. These are the ones that appeal to how the audience *feels*. Will they feel validated, surprised, or skeptical about the information you're sharing? Should they be concerned or fearful about not acting swiftly on this information? Can it serve them politically? Or does it respectfully stroke someone's ego?

My background is in advertising and marketing, and I can assure you that professionals in the industry know the formula for persuasion quite well. That's why babies have been used to sell tires, and investment brokers evoke images of middle-aged couples strolling carefree down secluded beaches. Remember, even the most rational number-cruncher isn't "moved" solely by the numbers, but by how he or she *feels* about those numbers (i.e., secure, satisfied, justified, relieved, respected, etc.). Whether you actually say in your presentation things like "be very afraid" or "you should feel outraged about this" is, of course, another choice you need to make in alignment with not only your objective for the audience, but the ongoing relationship you hope to forge with them. Just realize that current psychological research recognizes "emotions are the dominant driver of most meaningful decisions in life."* Knowing and acting on this wisely is where persuasion lies.

> *Remember, even the most rational number-cruncher isn't "moved" solely by the numbers, but by how he or she feels about those numbers . . .*

---

* "Emotion and Decision Making," Lerner, Li, Valdesco and Kassam, *Annual Review of Psychology*, June, 2014.

As we will see, it's also where your presentation storyline and dramatic energy often reside. So, remaining attentive to what you know and intend about the audience's emotional state (current and future) while developing your key messages can be very productive.

Next, prioritize your key messages. When you start combining, editing, and categorizing messages, the outline of a structure for your presentation begins to emerge. Some messages may end up being headlines or subheads in your presentation (more about these in the next chapter). The way you order them may suggest a flow to your presentation. Now it's getting interesting. You're starting to feel like you've "got" something. Great. Because you do! The strategy part (Steps One & Two) of your presentation planning is coming to an end, and you're at the tipping point where you are about to launch into tactics. But before you do, take a step back and ask yourself these types of questions:

> ▶ Are these messages all necessary and supportive of my strategic objective?
> ▶ Have I adequately addressed with these messages everyone I need to attend to in the audience?
> ▶ What more might I need to address and how?
> ▶ Will any of the messages (or omissions) be distracting to critical people in my audience?
> ▶ What could I say or do about this?
> ▶ Do they reflect the right balance of rational and emotional benefits given the audience and the topic?

▶ Are there any questions that are likely to come up in the Q&A?

▶ Should I address any of these earlier in my presentation?

Ideally, addressing questions like these now is better than deferring them to the rehearsal stage or a panic attack right before the presentation. It may even keep your visual aid preparation (or your staff's) from becoming a nightmare.

STRATEGIC EVIDENCE IS MORE COMPELLING EVIDENCE

Now that you know which key messages will form the skeletal structure of your presentation, you can move on to the last prioritizing question: *Which of these messages needs to be supported in greater depth and how?* In other words, what do I need to say, show, or do to give my audience reason to believe the benefits, logic, or urgency I've claimed?

Three things to keep in mind here: 1) PowerPoint and numbers aren't the only form of evidence you can use, 2) stick to the most compelling evidence tailored for your audience, and 3) remember that you will also carry weight as "evidence."

The following has been said before, and it's true. Power-Point and its cousins are mainstay tools of corporate America for which we are all grateful. Being schooled in their basics is essential, and lack of comfort with the technology can be unnerving and even a little embarrassing. However, the technology's sheer pervasiveness suggests an opportunity to be extraordinary by strategically deviating once in a while.

As a coach and trainer, I can assure you that things like stories, live testimonials, salient analogies, pictures, music, live demonstrations (other than the computer software variety)— and especially methods involving the audience in the most elemental ways—are still greatly underutilized in business presentations. So definitely entertain other options.

The key, of course, is keeping your choice strategic and compelling.

I'm not being a stick in the mud with this cautionary advice. As a person who once wrote a song, and sang and danced to it in a boardroom before a senior government audience to win an advertising contract, I'm hardly opposed to lightness and levity. Following on the heels of some good thinking, our entertainment addressed the prospect's wish that his agency contacts be the appropriate mix of smart business people and creative upstarts. We gave him reason to believe our claims that, indeed, we were that mix. And, yes, it gave us a whiz-bang ending!

On the other hand, some of you will remember a time when bullet points sweeping across the page with sound effects was innovative and different. At one point in the '90s, a consultant on a plane shared with me that the Pentagon had placed a moratorium on such special effects (mostly of the explosive variety) in briefings from contractors. For a Pentagon audience, whiz-bang apparently adds little to a presentation.

The moral of the story here is search your soul before you elect to do something "cool and different" as evidence for the audience under the guise that *they* are bored.

This is also a good place to remember that not everything has to go into your presentation. Some evidence can be placed in your leave-behind information or at the end of the formal set of presentation slides to be referenced as needed. Determining which evidence to include and which is only "nice to have" is a function of prioritization based on time available and the overall impact you wish to make. Need I add that, in an age of sound bites, less is often more?

> *The moral of the story here is search your soul before you elect to do something "cool and different" as evidence for the audience under the guise that* they *are bored.*

REMEMBER THAT YOU ARE EVIDENCE TOO

Finally, a word about *you* as evidence. The credibility factor is a huge piece of evidence that can't be overlooked. Credibility is something that is communicated not just by a résumé, but by how you sound, move, and look. Your pace, the way you use your eyes, even the way you interact with your visual aids are clues to the audience as to how competent you are to lead them through this information, this meeting, this decision, or crisis.

These are delivery issues that will be covered in greater depth in **Step Four: The How**. Suffice it to say here, however, that not leaving enough time to adequately rehearse can undermine even the best supported presentation.

Moreover, it can be deadly in a competitive situation. If you are using this process to plan a new business pitch, the end of this strategy phase of your planning (Steps One & Two) needs to include which presenters will best handle which messages. This is where egos need to be put aside and the best evidence needs to be put forward. Deciding who-will-do-what now will allow each presenter to adequately prepare and rehearse.

Now the time has come to move into the tactical phase of your presentation planning—what I call **The Way** and **The How**. If you've done a good job on the first two steps (**The Who** and **The What**), you should have a solid foundation to 1) efficiently map out your storyline in more detail and decide on the visual aids your audience needs, and then 2) practice a delivery style congruent with the experience you intend for that audience.

THE WAY

Map out your storyline first

THE WAY YOU decide to serve up your messages or tell your story has to do with structure. Audiences like structure. It lets them know that you have a purpose for the presentation and a plan for them. It keeps you on course, helps them follow along and, done correctly, can actually help them hold on to your message.

The tactical key is "doing it correctly." And, doing it correctly means *not* starting with the slides. Yes, that's what I said: no slides yet.

The first thing you need to do, preferably using pen and paper, is map out your story or plan for the audience. Once you have something that flows, then you can create the few compelling word slides or graphs that support that story or plan. In my training, I use a single-page flow chart tool that I call a QuickMap™ (not shown here). But you can use whatever suits you—even typing your thoughts into PowerPoint or Keynote one message per slide and re-arranging them as needed to create a flow. But be careful not to write a script or think of these notes as your actual slides for the presentation!

GOOD STRUCTURE: A PRESENTER'S RESPONSIBILITY

This single practice of first mapping out your storyline has the potential to separate the extraordinary business presenter from the merely ordinary. It's where presenters must exercise the most restraint and discipline to escape the lure of the ubiquitous PowerPoint briefing document that passes for the vast majority of presentations in business.

We all recognize the template structure of these so-called presentations. As I noted earlier, they usually begin with the presenter sitting down in front of a computer and first creating a Name and Title slide—something real compelling and topical like "Q3 Update." Then (if the audience is lucky) a Purpose slide is next, followed by a jam-packed Background slide that painfully rehashes every historical fact and extraneous bit of information about the company, product, service or issue at hand (just for level-setting). Then comes a long list of Topics that passes for an agenda, followed by every possible bit of information (in the form of charts) for each topic. Phew!

Finally, there is typically a Summary or Next Steps slide (no real conclusion, mind you, just a summary of stuff). The conclusion, if any, is usually conjured up in the eleventh hour as something that links the disparate mess of bullet points together. Otherwise, it's some variation of, "So that's the information. Any questions?"

We've all sat through many of these—and perhaps are guilty of a few ourselves. As audience members on the receiving end, we may be keenly aware of how mind-numbing they are and how they so often leave you with the burden of "connecting all the dots" yourself should you care enough. Yet, most of us persist in cranking out the same templates no matter the point or persuasive purpose at stake.

Fortunately, there is a better way.

That better way is to start with what you already have. If you've followed the steps so far, you already have a deep knowledge of your audience (both rational and emotional) and can articulate for yourself in detail what you want them to think, to feel, to do at the end of a particular interaction—be it a meeting, phone call, industry conference presentation, or WebEx. (Remember, all of these are presentations.) That means you already know the parameters of where you can reasonably start and where you need to end. Now, it's just a matter of mapping out the journey in between.

When it comes to organizing the components of your structure, I'm not going to tell you anything you haven't heard before. That's because there's a lot of sound communication research backing up the time-honored essay structure of Subject, Agenda, Body and Conclusion. If anything, I'm suggesting that you get back to being more disciplined—though a bit more artful—about it.

But it's not just about discipline for the sake of discipline. There's a definite upside in this for you. Good structure not only shows consideration for your audience; it's also the most obvious way in which you can demonstrate your leadership—by leading people effectively from a current mind state to a future mind state about you, the issue at hand, or about just having to be there.

Think of it as a way to gain credibility and provide persuasive evidence to an audience

> *Good structure not only shows consideration for your audience; it's also the most obvious way in which you can demonstrate your leadership.*

before even a single graph or chart is shown! You do this by signaling to them that you are prepared and have a plan that not only takes *them* into account, but also promises to deliver a productive and satisfying experience. No matter how thorny the issue at hand, this is the responsibility a presenter must shoulder to be most effective.

Since we're getting back to basics, let's first take a moment to understand the underlying way in which structure works, so that you can be more flexible and creative in your execution of it than you were in college.

Obviously, simply having a structure isn't enough. Fulfilling the underlying purpose of each part of a structure to best leverage your audience analysis and fulfill your objective is the more advanced goal here. It's time to get serious about those beginnings, middles and endings.

STRUCTURE IN THREE PARTS

In the Opening (which includes more than just subject and agenda), you transparently set your audience's expectations regarding the topic, or your point of view, plus the overall experience the audience can expect to have for the next however-many minutes they are in your care. The way you do this will vary, based on your audience analysis. In the Body, you deliver as promised on those expectations. Finally, in the Conclusion, you make sure that your audience got the messages you intended (and that you fulfilled your objective) by repeating salient points. Along the way, it's critical that you signal (with appropriate transitions) where you are in the structure to keep them apprised of your plan or storyline and how it's progressing.

Some of us may have learned a blunter variation of this structure that goes like this: 1) Tell 'em what you're going to tell 'em; 2) Tell 'em; and 3) Tell 'em what you told 'em. The repetition is intentional, because a lot of time can elapse between parts 1 and 3, and you want to make sure the audience members' wayward minds get to the same conclusion as you do in the end. A clear framing of the issues and context-setting up front, combined with selective repetition, are a means of helping the audience hold on to the information.

Any effective communication—short or long—tends to have such a three-part structure. Listeners may tolerate shorter communications that occasionally break this rule and make them work a little harder. They are less tolerant of meandering presentations that don't help them follow along or offer any reward for their patience (leading to bored disinterest or impatient hijacking of the presentation).

Most business presentations go awry because of these three common structural mistakes made by presenters:

> ▶ They don't set the expectations and overall tone for the interaction in their openings (i.e., frame issues, connect emotionally, or provide adequate context).

> ▶ They fail to hold that frame for their audience throughout the presentation.

> ▶ They conclude weakly.

Often, when I'm called in to provide coaching for an individual or team rehearsal—ostensibly on delivery issues only—these are the presentation components that end up having to be re-worked.

That's why at this stage, I'm going to focus primarily on the art of the presentation Opening. Nail this and the two other issues I noted above will be resolved easily. Let me give you a way of thinking about (and labeling) the components of an

Opening that is suitable for longer business presentations with a *persuasive purpose*. By the way, this should cover most business presentations. Why do them if not to influence a decision or outcome?

The goal here is to think of your Opening as a *map to guide your audience* from a *current* to a *future* state that is your desired think-feel-do conclusion.

THE ART OF THE OPENING

I can't emphasize enough the importance of how you open your presentation. This is where you must quickly connect with your audience, as well as share your plan or outline your story. It's where you usually make use of the emotional intel you have on your audience to either engage them or to help them set aside things that might get in the way of you being heard. It's about connecting with them, focusing their attention, and setting their expectations. If you don't do it here, the odds of you achieving your objective will be hit or miss.

The building blocks of a good Opening are the Logistics, Hook (if needed), Headline and Subheads (refer to the diagram on page 56). Here's an explanation of each and how to use them.

Logistics

Logistics are preparatory remarks, but I find that few people give serious enough thought to them. Most just rattle off their name and title and do an impromptu soft-shoe until they can find reason to jump into their first slide. Since this constitutes your first impression with an audience, the extraordinary

OPTIMIZE STRUCTURE TO LEAD YOUR AUDIENCE

A focused OPENING

Draw on your audience assessment to quickly connect, set expectations, and outline your plan or story. Talk to them directly, no slides required.

▶ **Logistics**—Address/answer anything that would distract them from listening.

▶ **Hook (optional)**—Consider ways to connect emotionally or pique their interest to focus them more precisely on your purpose.

▶ **Headline**—Start the conversation with statements that accommodate their current mindset and foreshadow where you intend to take them. Engage very direct audiences by stating your objective right here.

▶ **Subheads**—Outline 1–4 points you will use to lead them to your (yet unstated) objective or to confirm your (already stated) point of view. Use key messages and benefits here, rather than generic categories/topics, to convey a "storyline" that engages.

An organized BODY

Deliver as promised on expectations set in your Opening. Expand on each of the Subheads in order, supported by persuasive evidence. Don't forget to use . . .

▶ **Links**—to consistently remind the audience of where they are in your storyline or business case. (You can check in with your audience at these junctures to gauge their understanding/attitudes.)

▶ **Mini-agendas**—to itemize points and help them retain information.

▶ **Visual Aids**—to highlight the most compelling evidence that supports or illustrates key messages leading to your conclusion. Be selective.

A strong CONCLUSION

Again, no slide may be required. Tee up a collegial discussion or Q&A session by briefly recapping points and clearly articulating what you want them to feel—as well as think or do—about the issue or what they've just experienced.

speaker will take more care to lay the logistical groundwork for his/her audience.

Sure, most people may not be listening yet. But your purpose here is to settle them down, clear their minds of all that went before, preempt any questions they may have about you and your presentation that could be distracting, and generally just get them acclimated to you. It's your first opportunity to establish rapport with the audience by satisfying their needs and focusing their attention. Who wouldn't want to listen to such a considerate presenter?

This is where you might give a few relevant details about your credentials (i.e., not your full résumé, but why you have the right or a reason to be talking to them about the topic). It also never hurts to acknowledge others in the room and their contributions or points of view. You might also let them know how what you're about to say fits in (or contrasts) with what they may have heard prior to you speaking.

You could reference how long you'll be talking and when they'll get to respond. (This is a rare gift to the audience, because most speakers have no clue how long it will take them to "get through their slides.") If you know they're itching to ask certain questions, get a copy of the slides, see the numbers, or catch a plane—take a

> *Basically, the first words out of your mouth should be concretely for and about* **them.**

little time to be specific about how (and when) they will get what they need.

Your logistical comments should ideally give your audience whatever they might need rationally or emotionally right then and there—even if it's an explanation of what they *won't be* getting just yet—to help them focus and be more willing to give you the floor.

Basically, the first words out of your mouth should be concretely for and about *them*.

Hook (Optional)

This next component is optional, but worth a try if warranted, because of the impact and energy it can potentially generate with an audience.

In journalistic parlance, a Hook is a means of grabbing an audience's attention and focusing them more precisely on your purpose. In an essay, it would be called a "creative opening." Sadly, many of us think that nothing creative has a place in our business presentations, and for some audiences (remember my Pentagon story?), this may be true. But if you can think of an appropriate and creatively relevant way to focus an audience, it can give you a very strong start.

A Hook can take many forms—from a rhetorical question or little-known fact, to a story or interactive game, to even a highly produced video clip. Whatever form it takes, it should fulfill the purpose of focusing your audience's attention by *either* connecting with them in their *current (rational and emotional) state* or foreshadowing the *future state* to which you intend to guide them (see **Step Two: The What** for the discussion of objective-setting). Below are some examples.

If you know that virtually everyone in the audience is feeling overworked and underpaid, you may choose to connect with them emotionally by demonstrating that you understand their point of view. For example, you might recount typical laments overheard in the cafeteria and your own sincere frustrations of not being able to spend enough time with your family given the current workload. Your ultimate objective may be to re-assure employees that relief is on the way once sales goals are accomplished; but your audience analysis may have indicated that you need to do a more thorough job of showing you're listening, so as not to appear dismissive of their complaints. This is an example of using a Hook to speak to the audience's *current state*.

On the other hand, let's say you threw out a statistic—like 82%—and asked the audience what it meant. Perhaps there would be confusion and a few half-cocked answers and giggling before you satisfied their curiosity and explained it was how close they were to getting back to a normal workday! There may be some non-believers, but now you have them hooked. You can proceed to explain how you arrived at that conclusion and ask for their continued patience. In this scenario, the complaints and grumbling may have been vented enough in the past and the message now is "the end is near." Getting an audience to stop, take notice or be intrigued is often the purpose of foreshadowing the *future state* for your audience in your Hook.

Finally, a word about using humor—specifically a joke—as a Hook: unless you can both artfully tell a joke *and* accurately anticipate the audience's response, I usually don't recommend it as a first choice. The best humor arises out of a comfort with your audience that is pre-existing or earned in the course of the presentation. Lacking this, the result is often not an ice-breaker, but an icy silence. Not a good way to start a presentation.

> *The best humor arises out of a comfort with your audience that is pre-existing or earned in the course of the presentation.*

Remember, if you choose to use a Hook, it will be most successful if you can find a way to both "hook into" the audience's emotional state—present or future—*and* smoothly segue into the next component, which is your Headline.

Headline

I am loosely borrowing another journalistic term here to highlight the need in most business presentations to indicate clearly where you are starting the conversation with your audience.

A news headline doesn't just identify a topic ("The Economy"); but signals where the article is going with the topic ("Economic Indicators on the Upswing"). Likewise, a broad and indirect statement like "I'd like to talk about the Sales Meeting" may not be the strongest start for some audiences. Following are some important considerations when it comes to Headlines.

Consider the strength of your Headline. If your audience members are very to-the-point people, you may want to be more direct about your point of view and headline it with "I'd like to suggest that we move our sales meeting to Boca Raton." With a different audience, you may choose a more semi-direct statement like, "I recommend that we move the sales meeting to some place warmer and more accessible to our many Eastern corridor clients." Whatever your decision—even if it ends up being a more indirect headline, such as "I'd like to suggest location options for next year's sales meeting"—it should be determined by what you know about that audience's predominant approach to decision-making and any anticipated sensitivity to your suggestion.

The critical point here is that your objective (to sell Boca) may be the same in every instance, but your starting place (lead sentence or Headline) might need to be different based on where your audience analysis dictates you must start (and what you want them *to feel* about you and the whole interaction). This is especially important when you or your client is asked to take the same presentation to the next level of decision-makers.

This strategic grounding is the difference between the structure of a persuasive business presentation versus that of a college essay. In fact, with your audience clearly in view, there should be little risk of your presentations sounding too formal, generic or academic even though the underlying three-part structure may be consistent.

Subheads

The final step in setting expectations for an audience is to share with them the roadmap that you will be using to lead them to your conclusion. I recommend that you do this with

Subheads that are supportive of your Headline. That means the tried and true category section headings of Purpose, Background, Topics and Summary may or may not fit the bill here (probably not), since you've already started a conversation with your audience in the Headline. If you want it to *sound* like a persuasive conversation with the audience, the Subheads probably should take a form other than the typical agenda categories used in a briefing.

It's in the Subheads where the ordinary discussion of generic topics can be turned into a persuasive business "story."

For instance, suppose your Headline indicates that you will be recommending a relocation to some warmer climate for the sales meeting (a semi-direct approach). Your Subheads may begin with "Our Clients Would Prefer It"; then progress to "New Criteria for Locating the Meeting"; and end with "Say Yes to (TBD)!" where you promise your recommendation.

> *It's in the Subheads where the ordinary discussion of generic topics can be turned into a persuasive business "story."*

If, out of respect for certain important audience members, you decide to impartially discuss location options (a more indirect approach), you might begin with the "Pros and Cons of Meeting in Chicago"; then move to "What Our Clients Say" as being the real determining factor; and end with "A Short List We Can All Live With" that is strongly weighted toward Boca.

Finally, a more direct set of Subheads might be a few straightforward key messages: "The Chicago sales meeting venue no longer serves our purpose"; "Our clients' needs should be the determining factor"; and "Think Boca!"

For those of you who shrink from the thought of using such a direct approach as in this last example, think about this: There's nothing more frustrating for those direct and to-the-point executives (who already know that the general purpose of the meeting is to make decisions about next year's sales meeting) than to have someone get up and say, "I'd like to talk about the location of next year's sales meeting. But before I do, let's review where we've been and the pros and cons of each location." They're already looking at their emails until you get to the recommendation. Meanwhile, you're feeling like a voice in the wilderness up there. If you want to avoid this all-too-common outcome, make sure you base your tactical decisions—such as how you construct your Subheads—on the requirements of the audience.

Whatever your approach, the Opening of any presentation should reflect a forward-moving plan for your audience's consideration that indicates their time with you will be productive. That means productive in a way *they* think would be productive, whether it's putting a point of view out there and debating, outlining pros and cons and taking a person-by-person vote, or something in-between.

The key is to remember to share *all* the Subheads with the audience *before* you delve into the first one. Doing so will help listeners discern the seeds of your storyline or argument, if not your full conclusion. They'll know you have a plan for them and that they're probably in good hands. And, they'll be less likely to interrupt you—especially if you've already told them in the Logistics that you're only taking ten minutes, after which they'll get to speak. The real art in an Opening is in how it seems to be all about the audience, but ultimately serves to give you more control.

Crafting this type of Opening first (versus generating a bunch of supporting slides for a storyline that's yet to be articulated) has an added time-saving bonus for you. The Sub-heads? Those will likely become the headings for your slides (if you choose to use any). Now people can look at your slides after the fact and get the point by just reading the slide headings. Extraordinary!

Before leaving this discussion of Openings, I'll address a couple of questions that I often receive from my training participants.

> *The real art in an Opening is in how it seems to be all about the audience, but ultimately serves to give you more control.*

HANDLING COMPLEX TOPICS AND CANNED PRESENTATIONS

What if my content is complicated and I need more Subheads?

The complexity of your topic is no excuse for abandoning good structure. In fact, this is when structure is most critical. While you may need more than three points to advance a business case, my experience suggests that most of today's audiences can only hold on to three or four main messages at a time. So, try to prioritize your thoughts at this stage and expand on the details in the Body of the presentation. Check to make sure that you're not confusing the number of content items with the number of main points you have. For example, there may be a lot of qualifying considerations to acknowledge in making a decision about your topic. Rather than treating these each as separate Subheads, address them together by saying, "Finally, I will address some important considerations we'll need to keep in mind," then use an itemized agenda in the corresponding Body section to do so.

What if my company requires that I use a template for my presentation or, worse yet, I'm handed the slides I must use?

Ah, yes—the mandatory template or canned set of slides. This is often a futile attempt by managers to control time and messaging by imposing a framework that limits the number of speaker's slides. In fairness, they're only trying to help by giving you a *tactical* tool. It's still up to you to do the *strategic* part. That means stepping back and thinking about the audience you'll be talking to and formulating a think-feel-do strategy statement (Steps One & Two). Then, build the Opening frame as suggested here for which these slides will serve as "support" (or the Body of) your presentation. Nobody's controlling what you say before and in-between those slides. Focus on what framing and additional commentary would make these more relevant for your audience. That way, you're sure to be a more engaging messenger.

Trust me. The actual time spent in a presentation on an Opening may vary by situation and audience. But the leadership and respect that it demonstrates will be time well spent for all involved.

ARTFUL TRANSITIONING

Although the Body may be the longest part of any presentation, it should be the easiest to execute. Having already set clear expectations, now you just have to follow through on your plan to demonstrate what a trustworthy, confident and easy-to-follow leader you are. This is where you expand on and support each of the Subheads in your Opening with any additional key messages and persuasive evidence. Since you've already brainstormed these components, planning this part of your presentation is pretty much plug-and-play. Executing on it usually means just talking about what you know in an organized fashion and supporting it in the most compelling way possible.

From a structural standpoint, there are two main considerations here: the use of Links and Visual Aids. These are also delivery considerations (see **Step Four: The How**) having to do with bringing the structure alive for your audience, but I address them here for the reader's convenience.

Links

Links are the verbal transitions you use to connect each component in your map and guide your listeners to your conclusion. Smoothly bridging from a Hook to a Headline would be one example of a Link.

*Did you know that 35% of our east coast clients say they didn't sign up for last year's conference due to travel time required? **And these no-shows represent some of our biggest growth opportunities! That's why I'm here** to make a case for relocating the conference next year.*

However, smooth transitioning is also critical throughout the Body of your presentation. Links are what you use to hold the frame of your presentation for the audience.

> *What you should be linking is the storyline implicit in the Subheads, and not just repeating, "and on this slide what I wanted to talk about is . . . ."*

What you should be linking is the storyline implicit in the Subheads, and not just repeating, "and on this slide what I wanted to talk about is . . . ." You could say something as simple as, "Now let's look at what our clients have to tell us" to tee up where you're going. Or, in a longer presentation, a Link might be more like a stop-and-go signal such as, "So, it looks like we all agree the current meeting venue is no longer optimal. So where should we go? I suggest we let our clients be our guide."

It's not unusual for my training participants to ask for help with transitions as a development goal. Some training companies even offer "lists of transitions you can use." I find this to be curious, because all you have to do is link each Subhead section to the one before to keep the audience on track. As such, Links are considerate of the audience, because they remind them of the three to four Subheads you outlined in your Opening. More importantly, they allow you to explain your thinking as to why it's best they consider the information in this way. Therefore, they should *not* be generic, but helpful, conversational and particular to your storyline. So, if you're having trouble with transitions, or have received vague feedback from your manager that you "need to be more conversational up there," look to see if you have a story for your audience first.

FIND THE STORY IN THE NUMBERS OR DATA

I've worked with many finance and technical folks who would deny that such a story exists. They approach their presentations as if they are forever condemned to be boring presenters.

Certainly, I'd urge such clients first to reconsider *The Who* in an effort to discover and address what's at stake for their audience in all those quarterly numbers and flow charts they're presenting. From here, they can then build Subheads. But I'd also recommend that they simply be diligent about connecting the dots for the audience throughout the presentation as things get more complex. This means that if three charts together support the first Subhead, *tell the audience that*: "We're losing ground when it comes to our competitors and these next three charts hint at why."

Don't just plow through supporting data as if the people listening are tracking the argument. Maybe some are, but perhaps not all. And, don't presume they all read what you added in the "takeaway box" at the bottom of the slide (a classic case of burying your point). Say it out loud. It's just your job as a presenter, but your audience will experience it as extraordinary.

THE SUPPORTING ROLE OF VISUAL AIDS

These are my words of advice about including visual aids:

▶ Most of your visual aids belong here, in the Body of your presentation.

▶ By-and-large their purpose should be evidential—as in graphs, charts, quotes or illustrations that support Subheads and key messages that you speak to and preferably reference at the top of your slides.

▶ As noted before, make sure you have a storyline first, then go back and choose or create the visuals that will support that story.

▶ You *do not* have to have a slide for everything you say. Use your Opening and Conclusion to connect personally with your audience.

Of course, there is a case to be made for intentionally having the audience see and hear important words and information to better retain them. This implies an *infrequent* and *selective* use of bulleted information that actually aids the audience. In contrast, a litany of bullet points that serves as crib notes for the presenter only aids the hapless presenter and dulls the impact. And when a presenter assures me that "Oh, I don't actually say everything that's up there on the slide" so as not to be accused of reading the presentation, I can only pity his poor multi-tasking audience. (For more information on what to do instead, see the discussion in **FAQs: Applying the four-step process.**)

When it comes to visual aids, less is more. The structure, your plan and story for the audience, should be predominant. And it should largely issue from you, the presenter, if you wish to engage the audience and be viewed as a leader in that room.

CONCLUDING STRONGLY

The Conclusion is where it should all come together. By now the emphasis is on concise repetition and—if you haven't done so already—elucidating your persuasive point. You don't want to introduce any new information at this stage. You want to strongly finish the persuasive job you set out to do in your Opening. That means that you shouldn't do what 90 percent of business presenters do: conclude by simply listing Next Steps and saying, "Any questions?" This is especially true if the audience hasn't yet heard a clear articulation of your proposal or agreed to it.

If your Opening has three different Subheads, each supported by evidence in the Body of your presentation, then you should also have three summarizing statements in your Conclusion.

Do your best to make them succinct and easy to recall. The idea is not to rehash everything you've already said, but to help the audience walk away with an imprint of your key messages. Seek to either repeat or encapsulate your main message for each Subhead using the right level and tone for your audience (no slide may be necessary).

In summary, I hope you agree that we can do better than Chicago in March as a meeting location. While there are many considerations in choosing a location, I vote that we give priority to where the clients are. As I've shown, Boca could be very attractive.

But wait. You're still not finished. You can't jump into the Next Steps for planning the meeting relocation just yet. That may seem too presumptuous to your audience. Your think-feel-do objective still needs to be explicitly stated or repeated here in some way. Often, if you've largely summarized your rational proposal (what you want them to think), the conclusion may be a good place to expand more on the relational aspect of your objective:

So, to uphold our reputation as sponsors of the best confer-
ence in the industry, I ask that you consider re-locating the
sales meeting to the east coast next year and take a close look
at Boca. While it may require a bit more effort in the short
term, it could be a win-win for both our clients and us. But
if you have any doubts or anticipate any obstacles, let's talk
about those now, so we can work through them over the
next few weeks.

Note that if you've chosen to be very direct in your Headline (for a very direct audience), your Conclusion could basically be a repetition of that Headline, referencing any nuances that you may have elaborated on during the presentation. For example:

Headline: *I think it makes sense to double-down on our investment in proprietary software.*

Conclusion: *So that's why we should confidently stay the course and continue to pursue proprietary solutions in soft-ware that give us an edge. They're worth it.*

Finally, if you chose a very indirect headline in the Opening with your audience, just don't forget to ask for the sale, the money, the job, or whatever—when you get to the end. Never assume that it's patently obvious. The Conclusion is where you need to place a version of your objective squarely on the table to set up any ensuing discussion.

Congratulations! You've completed your course in the nuances and subtleties of mapping out a solid presentation structure from Opening to Conclusion. Ironically, if you want your presentation delivery to flow easily for the audience, you have to be rather anal yourself about outlining and rigorously connecting the dots for them.

Accept the fact that you probably won't do it perfectly the first time. Play with it. You'll find that this high-level mapping of your storyline is much more efficient a process than staring at a blank slide. Even better, if you take my suggestion and *talk through the flow at this early mapping stage* to find your Links—you'll discover and tweak any inherent problems in your flow right away.

> *Ironically, if you want your presentation delivery to flow easily for the audience, you have to be rather anal yourself about outlining and rigorously connecting the dots for them.*

This moves the process along much faster. Once you have this map, you can now note what slides need to be created. Odds are that you'll end up with fewer slides and a lot less aimless preparation.

Even better, on the day of your big presentation, if the gods are not with you, you will still be prepared. If the power goes out, or the projection unit breaks down, or the other presenters eat up half your time, you'll still have your map to aid both you and your audience. You'll still have something to say, *a cappella*. Extraordinary.

THE HOW

You should be their most important visual (and aural) aid

NOW THAT YOU'VE mastered the Way to structure your presentation, we can move on to the final step—determining How you want to sound and look to ensure that your message is received as intended. Neglecting to translate your plan from the written to the spoken word can be disastrous, and most experienced presenters have their war stories. Something always changes in rehearsal, so why not get the kinks out before you get in front of the client or the board? So many people are undisciplined about this stage that just taking this final step can be extraordinary.

Yet we avoid it for a reason: rehearsing can be frustrating and time-consuming. It's usually a painfully slow reminder that you're far from ready. I've seen estimates that range from three hours to one full day of rehearsal for every hour of presentation.

Ultimately, determining how much rehearsal is enough is a very personal decision that has to do with what it takes to get you reasonably comfortable and still (slightly) excited about the opportunity. It's the way you feel when you know you can swim, and are about to jump into the deep end of a pool in a competition. You're focused and all there.

WHAT CONSTITUTES REHEARSAL AND HOW MUCH IS ENOUGH?

Let's first look at what constitutes rehearsal—and what doesn't—and the most efficient way to incorporate it into your professional practice. Then, we can focus on key techniques you'll need if you want to deliver with that elusive quality called Presence.

First of all, if a presentation is important to you, rehearsal is a requirement. It's not something you do "if you have extra time." It's a professional discipline. Schedule it on your calendar *first* so that it won't be skipped. Then work backward to slot in the other three steps of the presentation planning process. (And as already noted, allot the most time to Step One, the audience analysis phase, from which all tactical considerations—structure and delivery—proceed.)

The goal of your presentation rehearsal is *congruence*. What you say and what the audience sees should match and project an overall sense of authenticity.

Rehearsal is the part where you physically embody the appropriate energy of your message—its tone of urgency, serenity,

> *The goal of your presentation rehearsal is congruence. What you say and what the audience sees should match and project an overall sense of authenticity.*

disappointment, apology, confidence, passion, excitement, etc. These are things that cannot be forced upon the audience or that need to be viscerally experienced by them to give them reason to believe you. Think of it as being physically behind what you are saying. How can an audience believe you or accept your proposal if you are trembling and stuttering or seem otherwise absentminded up there? Your behavior may have nothing to do with not believing in your own proposal. It may have more to do with inadequate rehearsal and delivery techniques. But as far as the audience is concerned, the result is the same.

The translation that occurs in rehearsal—from abstract ideas represented on a series of slides to the physical embodiment of your message—takes time. It takes longer for some than others, but time nonetheless. It implies that there is a point where you have to stop tweaking the slides and—as long as they're reasonably accurate and grammatical—just go with them and focus on your delivery instead. You have to be very honest with yourself here. Is your tweaking really making things that much better? Or are you just avoiding rehearsal?

REHEARSAL TIPS

The next rule of rehearsal is to do it *out loud*. Flipping through your slide deck in silence at the last minute does not constitute rehearsal. Your presentation just remains a mental abstraction. So get physical and try these rehearsal tips:

▶ As noted in the previous chapter, your very first rehearsal should be to yourself, talking through your storyline before you create any slides. This ensures that you have a story or business case or flow in the first place and greatly reduces the eleventh-hour tweaking of slides.

▶ For formal presentations and high-stakes opportunities, use a three-part rehearsal process of talk-through, walk-through and dress rehearsal.

▪ In a *talk-through*, you literally tell your story or state your argument out loud, making necessary adjustments and personal notes to your map. This is especially important when you are working with a co-presenter to make sure you complement each other's content and have smooth hand-offs.

▪ In a *walk-through* you actually get up for the first time and present with your slides or other visual aids, discovering and taking note of things—verbal and physical—that are working or need more work. Experience suggests that this could take up to three times the length of the actual presentation.

▪ Finally, in a *dress rehearsal* you try to simulate the actual presentation experience as much as possible. This usually involves timing yourself and making sure that you can get through the entire story—no matter what happens. No stopping to take notes or correct mistakes. Most of us need this under our belts to feel presentation-ready.

▶ Ideally, you should rehearse at least once in the actual room in which you'll be presenting. If this isn't possible, at least practice in a room roughly similar in size.

▶ Record yourself or get in front of a mirror to get a better sense of what the audience is experiencing.

▶ Better yet, present to a group of peers who know your intended audience and can be relied upon to give constructive feedback.

▶ If your job requires so many presentations that you honestly don't have time to rehearse them all, you'll have to prioritize the ones that matter most to you. For these, at least rehearse the Opening, Links (so you know the flow of information) and the Conclusion (to reinforce your objective). Consult **Step Three: The Way.**

YOU HAVE TO BE PRESENT TO HAVE PRESENCE

Rehearsal itself doesn't guarantee that you'll project Presence. Presence comes as a result of having a plan you are confident in (Steps One through Three), which allows you to have the presence of mind to be there for whatever actually happens in real time. Now that you're out of your head and connected to the audience, knowing a few good delivery techniques and when to use them will ensure that you deliver on your objective.

> *Presence comes as a result of having a plan you are confident in, which allows you to have the presence of mind to be there for whatever actually happens in real time.*

My goal here is to share concepts and techniques that are truly differentiating. While a couple may require additional rehearsal to create the "physical memory" required for them to become your default in a high-pressured situation, the result will be to make you appear more comfortable before an audience, no matter the situation. That comfort before a roomful of people who do not necessarily wish to trade places with you up there reads as confidence—and confidence is unquestionably an attribute of a leader.

FIRST, CONTROL THEIR FOCUS WITH EYE CONTACT

Eye contact is the most tangible way for a presenter to make what he or she is saying "about the audience." In this respect, it follows through on the most important tenet of effective communication. Eye contact should be a physical connection. When done properly in a group situation, it sends critical messages to the audience:

I know you are there.

I have something for you in particular.

I can see you and your response to what I am saying.

I want this to be a collegial exchange between us.

Giving the gift of attention to each and every person in your audience through eye contact is something that listeners tend to respond to in kind. They pay attention to you. Once established, this exchange of attention becomes your key to controlling their focus throughout the presentation. Do it

> *Giving the gift of attention to each and every person in your audience through eye contact is something that listeners tend to respond to in kind. They pay attention to you.*

from the start of your presentation, and they will likely choose to stay with you even when distracting slides are introduced. You will then have the ability to signal to them where to look and when. This is the extraordinary magic inherent in good eye contact. That's why I tell my clients to master this foundational technique of audience engagement first, before worrying if their slides are colorful enough.

There is a right way and wrong way to use eye contact in a group situation. We'll start with the wrong way that many of us were taught in school by instructors with all good intentions of quelling that ubiquitous fear of public speaking.

The wrong way often involves some variation of spraying your energy around the room with no particular target in mind. You generally look over people's heads or at the back of the room. You mentally divide the room into quadrants and each gets a sweep of eye contact. You rarely look at the people right in front of you because you are too busy holding forth to the group at large. You may also do this because it feels too intimate to look directly at those in front of you.

This approach leads to an uncomfortable sense of separateness and isolation for a presenter. You don't know how you're doing, because you are not really seeing how your audience is responding. And in the absence of this critical feedback, any and all fears about the situation start playing like a tape loop in the back of your mind. Whoops! You are no longer focused on the audience—you are focused on yourself and your fears—and not really present.

This same discomfort often leads to other common, but unproductive, tendencies:

▶ To skip using an Opening—with all its connecting benefits (see **Step Three: The Way**) so that you can quickly get involved with those more comforting slides instead of your audience.

▶ To speed up and strip your delivery of emphasis and impact in order to put an end to the ordeal.

▶ To zero-in on a single "friendly face" and ignore the rest of the room.

When you conduct yourself in any of these ways, the audience has no recourse other than to ignore you too. They look at their phones or chat with the person next to them—all of which you take personally. The tension inside you builds, and your experience of presenting as "something to be avoided" is reinforced.

Do yourself a favor and start practicing an eye contact technique favored by the most accomplished speakers. I call it *one-unit-of-thought-to-one-person*. It involves using eye contact to indicate to individual audience members the location of the natural pauses and punctuation of what you're saying. That means everything up to a natural pause—or to the next comma or period or dash—is conveyed to one listener at a time.

Keep in mind that where you choose to put the pauses and the punctuation will tend to be consistent with your unique vocal expression and intention for that audience. Here are some examples of what may be considered a unit of thought.

A unit of thought can be an entire sentence shared with *a single* audience member:

The only thing we have to fear is fear itself.

In this example, we can imagine this statement being experienced by the whole audience looking on as a simple, concluding truth.

Or, there could be two points of contact with *two separate listeners* as targets:

The only thing we have to fear . . . is fear itself.

Here, the experience of the audience may be more dramatic and inclusive due to the set up and punch line delivery used.

Conceivably, you could find three units of thought in this statement:

The only thing . . . we have to fear . . . is fear itself.

Depending on your use of voice, the impact of this delivery might be more consistent with a stern warning (slow and deliberate with perhaps added emphasis on *only*) or an epiphany (delivered with a building cadence).

There are probably delivery options as numerous as your creativity and particular context allow. However, the one you choose must always be consistent with your intention for that audience.

The simplest way to start mastering this skill is to deliver your thoughts in a way consistent with your punctuation. For example, just signal where the break is (at the comma) in this compound sentence:

(To Listener #1) *Let's take delivery on it now,*

(To Listener #2) *and we can worry about how to pay for it later.*

When you get good at it, you can begin to use your eye contact more strategically. That's when the words you choose to deliver to an audience member are particularly suited to that listener because of her role, function or known viewpoint. In the above example, Listener #1 is perhaps a proponent of immediate delivery; whereas Listener #2 has something to do with figuring out how to pay for it later. When you can do this, you are truly present to the audience.

> *When you get good at it, you can begin to use your eye contact more strategically.*

No doubt you can tell that this eye contact technique is more sophisticated and impactful than simply looking in someone's general direction for a count of three seconds. Here are some tips to getting it right:

▶ Make sure that you have a map for your presentation (See **Step Three: The Way**). When you know your intention for your audience, what your main points are and generally where you're going, the technique will come much more easily. When it becomes habit, you will be able to use it in impromptu situations as well.

▶ This technique requires that you get comfortable giving and receiving attention—often with complete strangers—through eye contact. It also requires that you proactively initiate that exchange of attention sooner (i.e., in your Opening), rather than later, if it's to happen at all.

▶ Some presenters find this exchange of attention unsettling—so much so that I sometimes do an exercise in my training that involves *looking in silence* at a partner for three minutes at a stretch to become more accustomed to the experience. (Yes, blinking is allowed. It's not a staring contest.) If eye contact is a larger than normal obstacle for you, ask a willing colleague to do this exercise with you. Otherwise, just work on the technique when you're presenting to an audience you are comfortable with at your next Monday morning update. No one has to know, and you'll be preparing yourself for your next high-stakes presentation.

▶ The technique works even when you're speaking to a group of five hundred. The good news is that you *do the exact same thing* you would do in a meeting room with five people. In a large group, perspective will work for you: even though you still deliver a thought to just one person, about five to eight people around that person will swear you are speaking to them. This is how you work the room! So make sure that you pick out different people, not the same four points in the room. Use the same technique, no matter the audience size.

▶ The more units of thought per sentence, the more energetic and dynamic the delivery can become. This usage of the technique is particularly suited to conveying passion and energy to whip up an audience. But don't tire them all out. Save this for the crescendo or parts that really are exciting.

▶ Alternatively, if your nervousness expresses itself in rapid delivery, use this technique very mindfully to slow yourself down (more on this in the section on pausing).

▶ Many of us have trouble looking at someone and thinking at the same time. The truth is, you don't have to be looking at someone every second—just a whole lot more than you're looking at your notes or your slides.

▶ Keep in mind that there's nothing wrong with using notes—they indicate that you have a plan for the audience. Consult them silently and deliberately in a way that shows everyone you are making sure you've shared all the important information you have to offer. This conveys leadership presence. Don't "sneak a peek" at them as though you are scattered, forgetful and apologetic. This screams "I'm nervous and in my head." Like a lot of things in life, part of leadership presence is in the recovery, as opposed to performing perfectly all the time.

GET COMFORTABLE WITH THE PAUSE

As we've seen earlier, it's an easy segue from eye contact into issues of vocal delivery. That's because the *one-unit-of-thought-to-one-person* technique creates *pauses*, and pauses create the space where you can put your voice to good use for the audience.

Unlike a voice coach who focuses on breathing and vocal range, as a communication coach I tend to focus on the *range of effects* you can create with your voice that are consistent with your objective for the audience. That said, you gotta breathe! We have all heard that deep breathing does wonders

> *The* one-unit-of-thought-to one-person *technique creates pauses, and pauses create the space where you can put your voice to good use for the audience.*

for calming us and getting oxygen to our brains so we can think clearly. These effects play no small role in contributing to overall presence. Making space for that to happen is certainly important for you. But let's consider it from the audience's perspective.

One of my greatest disillusionments as a listener happened when I visited the American Cemetery & Memorial in Normandy, France. Make no mistake, if you want to get a visceral sense of history regarding the sacrifice and poignancy of a not-too-distant war that hugely impacted our Western way of life,

I can recommend no better place to spend a day. It is a treasure and a tribute to the human struggle. I had one small disappointment, however; and that was with the voice of General Eisenhower.

Everything about this place causes you to have a lump in your throat. When you walk in, there is a famous quote from Eisenhower's address to the troops launching the D-Day invasion, emblazoned on the wall like the words of an oracle: *The eyes of the world are upon you.*

As I made my way through this highly interactive museum—eager to hear and see with the greatest possible verisimilitude what my parents and grandparents had known—I was presented with the option to listen to the D-Day address as the troops had heard it. I pushed the button. Out came a whiny, clipped rendition of a pre-written statement that sounded like, "Blah, blah, blah, The-eyes-of-the-world-are-upon-you, blah, blah, blah."

Alas, what had been excerpted for the history books was in reality delivered as a throwaway line. It was as though Eisenhower had no real sense of the gravity of the moment. (Odds are that he did and was perhaps trying hard not to be fully present to it.) Nonetheless, he delivered it like a platitude from a high school basketball coach at halftime, instead of like a Leader of the Free World on the precipice of a do-or-die moment.

What I experienced was an emotional incongruity that just gets in the way for a listener. It colored everything I saw and heard thereafter about Eisenhower. In my training, I often ask my participants to deliver typical business throwaway lines (e.g., "We have to make every meeting count!") in different ways. Invariably, when delivered quickly, the group's interpretation has to do with how upset and frazzled the presenter is. When delivered slowly, all agree it becomes key message material: *We. Have. To Make. Every. Meeting. Count.*

What happens is that the deliberate speed and intentional pausing lends a weight or gravity to the words. We hear this shift in speed as emphasis, and emphasis means it's important. It's also not unusual for the participants doing my exercise to suddenly start using deliberate eye contact and corresponding gestures when they slow things down. Why? Because they're creating the spaces where such accenting behaviors have room to happen. All of these together serve to make the message pop.

The moral of the story here is not to always be dramatic and affected. However, I do recommend that you at least a) know your key messages, and b) when you get to them—put some air in and around them. The shift in cadence will be experienced by the audience as a signal to look and listen. Mission accomplished.

But as the Eisenhower anecdote suggests, another extraordinary benefit of getting comfortable with the pause is in the space it allows for emotional content. As stated earlier, the emotional impact that our listeners experience is as much a product of *how* we say things as the words we use. And, there is no better tool for delivering on our emotional messages than voice. More than any of the other delivery skills, voice conveys the most emotion and meaning.

Do not overlook this most highly effective tool in your possession. One way to make certain you don't is by making the out-loud rehearsal a part of your professional discipline. This will give you a chance to calibrate the emotional content of your message and wear it more precisely for your audience.

I have focused on the *absence* of sound in this discussion on voice. That's because in all those situations where a presenter needs to start and stop the verbal flow, *pausing* is the control mechanism. It is the ability to start and stop things with a purpose at important junctures:

- between the Opening and the Body
- between the Body and the Close
- to signal a shift in emotional tone
- to quickly review things that are already known
- to add weight or gravity to things that deserve focus
- to ponder a rhetorical question with an audience
- to indicate you are seriously reflecting on a person's question

Granted, knowing your audience and having some emotional context—plus a clear objective and a structure to put it in—precede the need for this control mechanism. Without these, pausing—like eye contact—is just a technique. But when you put it in the service of accomplishing the various purposes outlined above for your audience, it becomes strategic. All those worries about modulation or sounding too monotonal that are usually part of a discussion on voice become moot points.

So, embrace the dead air! Enliven it with purpose!

And, should a pause occur because you just had a mental hiccup—look at your notes *deliberately*. Then, reconnect with your audience using the eye contact technique. Doing so will better serve to underscore the additional or corrected information you're sharing.

> *Embrace the dead air!*
> *Enliven it with purpose!*

Whatever you do, resist the urge to go into performance mode and apologize because you missed your triple axel. They didn't know it was coming anyway. Take your time (you know this stuff). Don't give up your power to the fear of dead air. Take it back. That's a purposeful pause. That's *Presence*.

MOVES YOU CAN USE WITH PURPOSE

None of the delivery skills are approached with as much hesitancy and studious avoidance as movement. That's because it's the most misunderstood. As I see it, however, this sets up an opportunity for the ordinary business presenter. If you incorporate effective movement into your presentation repertoire, it will scream both confidence and extraordinary leadership presence.

At its root, hesitancy around movement is really just a variation on the fear of pausing. The problem is that the "dead air" associated with going from point A to point B can feel really long and obvious to an anxious presenter.

Movement should be intentionally used as a visual pause. Purposeful movement means you are indicating that something is ending and something new is beginning. It requires that you be very deliberate and know where you're going. If you're not, it can appear hesitant and weak—the exact opposite of what you should be projecting. In the face of this risk, the ordinary presenter either avoids movement altogether or blathers through it until it becomes no more than nervous fidgeting.

Here are some simple guidelines for incorporating the power of purposeful movement into your next presentation. Though they may seem formulaic, the reality is you don't have to be overly animated to hold an audience's attention. A few key moves that *coordinate with the structure or map for your presentation* can accomplish things quite nicely. So let's get comfortable with three basic moves you can use with purpose in a typical business presentation.

> *If you incorporate effective movement into your presentation repertoire, it will scream both confidence and extraordinary leadership presence.*

Up and Down

We all know that we need to stand up to be seen in a formal presentation in front of a large audience where we are the designated speaker and focal point in the room. But the vast majority of business presentations are in small meeting rooms in front of only three to ten people sitting around a table. For this reason, and because we'd like to project an air of comfort and casualness, we tend to sit. The justification for not using (or learning about) movement becomes "I don't do many formal presentations."

The first rule is to throw out the rules about "standing = formal" and "sitting = casual." There are many "formal" board presentations delivered sitting at a table and many "casual" meetings where you certainly want your ideas to still be the focal point in the room. The only real rule is to do what is necessary to focus the attention of the audience so that they can take in your ideas more easily. That's where "up and down" movement with purpose can help. Consider this common scenario:

It's your turn to present your project update in a casual team meeting and no one else has been standing so far. Most presenters are reluctant to stand up and act like they're taking over. It seems too awkward. But consider this: At that moment, it *is* your meeting; and you *are* responsible for controlling the focus and outcomes for that audience.

Yes, it might be awkward to pop up without warning and start holding forth. So what you can do instead is deliver your Opening (see **Step Three: The Way**) from a seated and slightly forward position, making sure you establish good eye contact with each and every person around the table. During this Opening, you perhaps share your plan with the audience that you're going to take five minutes to review some information with them on a few slides, after which you'd like to hear their feedback.

Once you've done this, you can now stand without anyone being startled or questioning your motives. When you're done with your slides, you can sit (for your Conclusion) to signal that you are now receptive to all their points of view.

You could stand up just as easily when showing evidence to support just one critical point, as long as you forewarn them. They may not agree with you or may be jealous of your leadership presence, but no one will question the efficacy of how it was delivered. It just made sense and was helpful.

Side to Side

Side-to-Side movement is usually reserved for delivering transitions. Phrases like "Moving on to our next issue" or "But let's look at it from a different perspective" present natural opportunities to move across your stage—even if it's only a couple of steps at the front of a meeting room table. Your movement inserts a visual respite from the flow of important key messages that signals something is ending and something new is beginning.

This side-to-side movement can work for everyone in the room. Your audience needs this time to process information, take a note or formulate a question. You need it to think about where you're going or to look at your notes. And remember, if you want to really grab the attention of your audience, move without saying a word. The absence of sound will cause everyone to look up expectantly to hear what's coming next. The comfort with the pause that you'll project will be extraordinary.

Back and Forth

This pattern of movement is typically reserved for interacting with visual aids—the only purposeful reason you'd have to back away from the audience. The net result is that you stay close to the audience when you're in your storyline and only go back to the visual aids when you want to direct their focus there. When you're done with a particular slide, you come back to the audience to continue your storyline or set up the next slide you will show them (and eventually interact with).

This approach ensures that the *audience is your primary focus* as a presenter and the slides are something *you lead them to* at the appropriate time to support whatever you are telling them in that moment. (For more on how to effectively interact with visual aids see, **FAQs: Applying the four-step process**.)

On a larger stage, these movements will take more steps and can add a bit of dynamic energy to your presentation. In a room where the space between you and the audience is small, your movements will be correspondingly small—but no less effective.

The above movement guidelines should always be used to make the audience's experience easier and more productive. But the subtle benefits that accrue to you as a result of perfecting this delivery tool cannot be denied. First, any nervous energy you brought into the room tends to dissipate when executing purposeful movements like the ones I've described. Secondly, movement forces you to use your *physical presence* to control the focus of the audience, making you their most important and memorable visual aid. Yet another reason to make time for that rehearsal!

USING DELIVERY TECHNIQUES STRATEGICALLY

Obviously, delivery techniques like eye contact, pausing and movement are easier seen and heard than read about, and I encourage you to revisit these skills with training or coaching at different junctures in your career—especially when your audiences change or become more diverse. But the understanding of why you're doing what you're doing will help you make better choices before and during your presentations. It's the mark of a true professional.

A final word of caution: please don't mistake simply knowing and using delivery techniques with being an extraordinary presenter. We all know people who can appear very "smooth" and confident in front of an audience, but over time are revealed to be very light on content and strategy. They're called one-trick ponies. The difference often has to do with experience and intentionality.

Please don't confuse simply knowing and using delivery techniques with being an extraordinary presenter.

I have observed that the less experienced participants in my training tend to be focused on delivery techniques. This is understandable. All of us need to learn what constitutes *acceptable* behavior so as not to embarrass ourselves up there. But confusing this with being a good presenter is a sure path to a middling performance.

More accomplished presenters tend to get into the strategy of a presentation. A light bulb goes on when they see that the key to their success lies in continuously focusing on their audience from the planning stage all the way through to the physical delivery of their presentations. The entire process becomes a professional discipline. Delivery techniques are just tools to be practiced and deployed when needed in a way that is scaled to their intention for that audience. Always staying connected to that "intention" (Step Two) becomes the focus for these *extraordinary* presenters.

FAQs

Applying the four-step process

B Y NOW YOU know that the process outlined in the previous chapters is simple in concept, but rich in its implications. It embodies a practice to which you as a professional must bring the discipline. The discipline required of most business people usually has to do with the following:

- Doing the steps in the order outlined
- Spending enough time analyzing your audience in a way that yields actionable implications
- Articulating a thoughtful think-feel-do strategy statement from your audience's perspective
- Mapping out your storyline *before* you create any slides
- Scheduling enough time to rehearse

My advice is to start by applying this process to your biggest opportunities first to ensure the best outcomes possible. You will undoubtedly still have room for improvement, but you will not have wasted your effort or the opportunity. Over time, the tactical techniques will become second nature, and you'll find yourself spending more upfront time on audience analysis questions and detailed objectives to guide you more quickly through the development of any presentation, big or small.

Advancing beyond a merely presentable performance to something consistently exemplary and productive for all takes honing and effort, but has its own reward. It is a differentiator that tends to propel careers. It doesn't come as a result of picking up a tip here and there, but by grasping the underlying reason as to why you're really up there presenting. I hope that, rather than "giving you a fish" that will get you through one stressful presentation, I have taught you "how to fish" with a method that will serve you for an entire career. That said, you might have some outstanding questions that haven't yet been addressed.

> *Advancing beyond a merely presentable performance to something consistently exemplary and productive for all ... has its own reward. It is a differentiator that tends to propel careers.*

AT MINIMUM, OBSERVE THESE RULES OF ENGAGEMENT

I get a lot of similar questions from my training participants as they work to make the practice their own. Often, the
answers are inherent in the process itself once you get comfortable with the underlying principles on which it is based. In my
training, I call these the Rules of Engagement; and they represent a summary of all that's been discussed so far in this book:

▶ Plan your presentation or interaction starting from your
audience's perspective. Make it about them as quickly as
possible if you want to be engaging and effective.

▶ Don't overlook your listeners as emotional beings. The
emotional dynamic in the room could be the obstacle
to you being heard as well as the key to persuasion and
motivation. Remember, in any communication there are
at least two considerations: the content or what's being
discussed and the relationship with the listener(s). Take
responsibility for both in any interaction, but at the very
least make sure you salvage the relationship and connect.
This will better ensure that you can engage again on the
content at a later time.

▶ Audiences need structure. So use it—and clue your audiences in on it—to make it easier for them to take in and
remember your messages. It's not enough to give them a
list of topics you want to talk about. (That's *your* agenda.)
Tell them *why* you're doing what you are doing and how

it benefits them. Then make sure you hold that structure for them by consistently reminding them where they are in the structure throughout your presentation.

▶ You are the most important visual aid in the room. Use everything available to you—eye contact, voice, movement, etc.—in a way congruent with your purpose and you will not only control their focus, but also project confidence, authenticity and presence.

Many of the remaining questions I field in my training and coaching sessions have to do with "What do you do when . . .?" or "What is the rule of thumb for . . .?" Admittedly, some tips come as a result of experience, and I'll share some of those here. But many times, the answer goes back to more strategic considerations that almost make the question seem off-base. Here is a sampling of such questions offered as guidance. Once you get the hang of the four-step process and its audience-centered approach, you should be able to answer these and more for yourself and your colleagues.

I don't formally present, I just review information in meetings—sometimes just one-on-one. Any advice for effectively communicating in meetings?

Anytime you are putting forth ideas in a purposeful way counts as a presentation. It can be to one person or many. You can be in a meeting, on the phone, on an interactive Internet site, answering a question after a scripted presentation, or in an

> *Anytime you are putting forth ideas in a purposeful way counts as a presentation. It can be to one person or many.*

interview, etc. When you think about it this way, your strategy should be much the same as we've discussed. You can then apply the tactical techniques available to you depending on the format you're working in (see the following question for an example).

Other than this, the next most important thing to do if you're leading a meeting (or your portion of a meeting) is to take responsibility for having a plan for that interaction. You should share it, as well as the proposed outcome (not just an agenda of topics), with everyone present *before* you launch into talking about stuff. (Refer to the earlier discussion on **The What** and **The Way**.) This is what gives your listeners a sense that you've thought about how to make this time productive for them. They can now tacitly or verbally agree to cooperate with you in the meeting. And, if they don't, you should revisit the plan together. Most listeners don't willfully hijack meetings. They do it in the absence of a plan—or they simply forget what you said and need to be reminded of it politely by you or the others participating. When meetings go awry and turn into a free-for-all, it's usually because there is no leader with a plan.

I do most of my presentations remotely via teleconferences or WebEx where eye contact and movement aren't useful. What should I do to be engaging in these formats?

It's a sad truth that most business people have come to view these meeting formats as an opportunity to multi-task. Your meeting often becomes a background radio program that is getting only half their attention at best. Unfortunately, these less than optimal formats are unavoidable in an increasingly global business environment.

In the absence of visual cues, you must work with what remains—structure and voice—and really amp these up to create anything close to the kind of engagement possible in a face-to-face meeting.

From a structural perspective, you should be very explicit regarding the goal for the interaction. Be step-by-step specific with your listeners about what's going to happen to achieve the goal and how much time you will spend to accomplish each step within the given timeframe.

Even more importantly, *give the listeners very specific things to do.* Most of us recognize the need to make it interactive, but often we don't know how to do it. We throw questions out into the void and are met with the dreaded "dead air" that we end up filling ourselves to relieve the tension. This is where the type of vocal control discussed in **Step Four: The How** can be critical to your success.

For example, if you want to get colleague feedback on a proposed process that you are in favor of implementing, don't just say, "I want to tell you about an exciting process that I want your feedback on" and launch into it.

Instead, consider your audience strategy first. Will they think your process is indeed exciting and the answer to all their problems? Or do you have to take a more pros and cons approach and anticipate pushback? After you assess where to begin with your audience and formulate your strategy about what you want them actually thinking, feeling and doing, you are ready to share your plan. You might tell them that you will take ten minutes to review the pros and cons as you see them, and that as you do so, you'd like them to consider three questions: What do they see as the benefits to the new approach? What are the roadblocks? How might any roadblocks be avoided? You can even say that you will be asking them individually for their opinion. Now they've been forewarned.

When you finish your ten minutes, you can return to these questions, ask who would like to begin, and be silent. Remember, you may have to exercise comfort with the pause here. Most listeners aren't used to having anything actually happen on these calls, much less having to do something. Initially, you are getting them acclimated to a new way of doing things. So, hold your silence and put the onus and tension on them. Soon, you'll hear them jumping off "mute," and you'll be back in business.

Finally, consider these additional tips for sustaining engagement in virtual meetings:

▶ At minimum, rehearse your Opening to ensure a forward momentum in the flow of ideas for the meeting and to keep up your own energy.

▶ Use a co-presenter (as a co-anchor) to help vary what the listeners hear or to provide color commentary.

▶ Stand up yourself, move around and use gestures to support your own energy. Even if the teleconference audience members don't see your movements, your energy will be transmitted.

▶ Bring in a small audience of interested parties and use your eye contact technique, so that you sound like you're talking to someone. In a pinch, do what a friend of mine who was a radio personality did: set up photos of people you know in front of you, and talk to them.

The executive sponsors of my project have deep disagreements regarding how to proceed. I can hardly get through my status updates. What can I do?

The first issue to address is your own assessment of the situation. You may see your job as giving a status update, when what's really required is that you facilitate the tension in the room in the most collegial way possible. Simply put, the audience is not ready for a status update. An update assumes that there is a set of agreed upon expectations to report on—which doesn't exist. The underlying consensus needed to go forward is what your meeting should be about. That's the discussion that will be most productive.

If your audience analysis tells you that springing such an honest discussion on this audience publicly will not be well received, you can consult with the parties individually to come up with a plan for addressing the real issues in the room. Make them your partners in solving the problem. Stay above it—respect all the points of view in the room and make it possible for them to resolve it themselves when they see the impasse it creates. This is an approach that is routinely used at the board level when dealing with strong personalities and opinions in the room. The next time a simple update reveals that there's much more going on, see it as an opportunity to gain a reputation for using board-level savvy in conducting your meetings.

My boss gave me a few slides to present at the senior management meeting. They are just informational in content. How can I improve my delivery?

By all means rehearse and use good techniques like the ones discussed in **Step Four: The How,** and you'll comport yourself well. But I always challenge my clients to be more strategic in these situations. Your boss is offering a chance for you and senior management to get better acquainted. What impression do you want to leave? Maybe you want them to think that you get the bigger picture and to feel that you grasp what is at stake. Perhaps, you'd even like them to come to you about this issue when your boss isn't available. But resist concluding that this is your strategy statement, because these concerns are still all about you.

Instead, reflect on your boss's goal for the meeting and how what you're sharing must contribute to that goal. Speak to it succinctly in your Opening and envision your role as helping management easily grasp the issues through the evidence you're presenting. Focus on and speak to the confidence, transparency, insight or concern you need to be igniting in your audience. Say and look as though you welcome any questions they might have. If you're worried about this part, strategize with your boss in advance so he or she has your back.

Don't just repeat the information on the slides. You will only achieve your goal of maximizing the opportunity given to you by focusing on what needs to be accomplished for your boss and management. You'll look and sound like you are part of the conversation. That's how delivering a few ordinary slides can have an extraordinary impact—for your audience and you.

I'm fine during my presentation, but get nervous about Q&A. How can I do better at thinking on my feet?

The fear of going off script and having to face the unexpected or dreaded question runs deep with many presenters. It's when we get hard on ourselves and wish we could just wing it, like we've seen some other colleagues do so confidently. However, Q&A should be just an extension of the conversational relationship you initiated at the beginning of your presentation. As such, consider these tips and action items:

> *Q&A should be just an extension of the conversational relationship you initiated at the beginning of your presentation.*

▶ Unexpected questions usually come from listeners we don't know well or points of view we didn't anticipate. During your preparation process, ask yourself if you've done as much as possible to anticipate the needs and attitudes of the audience and to accommodate these in the course of your presentation. Even if you didn't anticipate everything (and no one really can), your listeners should sense your effort to be thorough and accommodating. Their appreciation will be reflected in the collegial tone they use in respectfully raising an additional issue. In this way, Q&A shouldn't be viewed as a game of "stump the speaker."

▶ If there's a reason you avoided addressing an issue or chose not to make it part of the scope of your presentation, disclose this in your Opening; otherwise, it could become a nagging distraction for some in the audience. This is a matter of being respectful of your audience members as thinking individuals. Help them set the matter aside until later.

▶ You likely already know what the most dreaded questions will be, so rehearse and be ready for them. Treat them as mini-presentations that have a think-feel-do strategy attached to them.

▶ Finally, calmly and intentionally sit down to answer questions, i.e., don't slink into a chair or rush as you're finishing your last sentence. Close your presentation with strong eye contact, give it a few beats and then settle into a receptive posture. This signals that you are taking yourself out of presentation mode, having already shared everything you know about an issue. When you combine this with a spoken invitation, posture and attitude that indicate, "I want to hear what you have to say now," the tension in the room (mostly yours) can be better managed.

What if I don't know the answer to a question?

It happens. The fact is, we usually know so much more about our audience's needs *after* we have encountered them. It's how relationships grow and trust develops over time. So, if you really couldn't give them what they wanted or needed this time, make salvaging the collegial relationship your paramount concern. At least let them know that you sincerely wish you could answer their questions and intend to do everything possible to remedy the situation.

Whatever you do, don't slip into "failed performance" mode where you say nothing, become downcast and disengaged, or bluster apologies and excuses. Instead, get really interested in their questions as an equal. Listen intently and validate their queries. If there is discussion, make it sound like a discovery of where your assumptions may have diverged. ("I see. I was assuming that this would occur later in the process, whereas you're pointing out that it could, in fact, occur earlier and that we'd better be prepared for it.") Your thoroughness here will make the questioners feel heard and (almost) as satisfied as if their questions had been answered. Relationship saved.

What if they interrupt me before I've made my point or concluded my argument?

There are a few false assumptions embedded in this question that must first be made transparent:

- ▶ that questions are an interruption
- ▶ that a presentation is a one-way monologue
- ▶ that the presenter has no control over the situation
- ▶ that you can assume everyone will politely wait for you to get to your point

Questions should be a signal of audience engagement and treated as such. When they are not—if they are demanding and off-base—perhaps we haven't done everything we could to turn the one-way monologue they're objecting to into something they feel is a first step in a valuable exchange that might benefit them.

The assumption that presenters should be able to talk until they get to their last slide, after which questioners interrogate them to extract what they each need from the presentation, is all too common. In fact, it represents an abdication of the presenter's responsibility as a leader in that moment.

This whole book is about how to reinvent that adversarial experience into something productive and beneficial for everyone in the room.

There's more than one way to do it. Frankly, I prefer and usually make time for questions to be asked in the course of a presentation. This helps me know how I'm doing and gives me an opportunity along the way to make sure my audience is still with me. But, it's always the presenter's responsibility to share the way the interaction will flow with the audience and to gain their agreement. This involves being aware of your audience's tolerance for explanation and listening. If these are not their forte—due to their personalities or the pressure and demands of the business—then you must create a forum that is effective for them. In this case, engage them by getting to your point quickly; provide only the most compelling evidence; and spend the rest of the time answering their questions until they are satisfied. Thus, we return to the first rule of engagement: make it about them.

How much time should I devote to my Opening? My entire presentation? Or Q&A?

It may sound flippant, but the answer is that you should allow as much time as needed to accomplish your strategic goal for that interaction.

Your Opening should be long enough to establish a relationship with your audience, clear their minds and focus them on your plan. This can be done in short order with a familiar audience. But, if you are introducing change, addressing an audience for the first time, or positioning a highly emotional topic, it could take more time.

Your presentation should be no longer than what's needed to tee up a good conversation about the issue at hand. So, if you sent out the deck of slides in advance, don't belabor what they've already seen—position your point of view strongly and get on with the conversation. Finally, the Q&A should be enough time to have whatever productive dialogue is required to advance the conversation, decision or project.

If you think of your presentation as the first salvo in a dialogue with your meeting audience, then a fifty-fifty split is a good rule of thumb. The next time someone gives you thirty minutes at a department meeting to make your case, plan on fifteen minutes for content and you'll be in good shape. You can stretch that to twenty minutes, or two-thirds of the allotted time as a maximum, if the content is completely unknown to your audience and they are relying on you for guidance. Even then, though, you'll want to allow adequate time to find out what they're getting or not getting from what's been said—as that will be the measure of your success.

> *The next time someone gives you thirty minutes at a department meeting to make your case, plan on fifteen minutes for content and you'll be in good shape.*

Is it possible to over-rehearse?

Because avoidance of rehearsal is a time-honored form of procrastination, I am reluctant to discourage it in any way. However, it is true that you can over-rehearse. It occurs when you move from a fresh engagement with your content and the audience to a mere memorized recitation of words. People who are very anxious about presenting are most prone to it. Having too much content to fit into a small amount of time can prompt it as well.

The lack of situational awareness that results from this state usually manifests as a rushed or flat vocal delivery and, worse, saying and doing incongruent things (like introducing yourself robotically after you've already been introduced, repeating information already stated, an inability to respond naturally to unplanned interruptions, not seeing questioners, etc.) In short, over-rehearsal can throw you back into your head and into performance mode.

But it's not a one-way ticket either. As anyone who has had to return to an old presentation or roadshow a few weeks later has learned, rustiness can set in pretty quickly. So, learn your own "fill line" at which point content recital becomes unthinking and the upcoming opportunity becomes boring. Then it's time to step away and reconnect with your purpose for that opportunity and for that audience. On the day, you'll probably just need to review your Opening and your Links. The connection and content will flow from there.

What if there are technical problems or my time gets cut short?

Learning to use your technology should be part of rehearsal. It's especially important when you're selling that technology or its ease of use. However, technology failures and hiccups can be beyond your control and don't have to be deal-breakers.

Likewise, it's a common occurrence for speakers scheduled at the end of a meeting agenda to get cheated on time.

In either of these situations, you should be able to rely on your intention for your audience and the map of your ideas or flow for the interaction. You should know your key messages and (in the event of technology failure) be able to articulate, draw or list your most compelling evidence to support them. Likewise, you should be able to skip to your most pertinent slides if you are short on time. That should be enough to tee up a conversation. Perhaps you end up using ten minutes instead of fifteen or twenty as originally planned. No one will ding you. In fact, you'll be a hero. And if the time remaining could not possibly give the topic its due, then claim your right to your thirty minutes and move it to another time.

What if my presentation is a technology demo and the technology is the real centerpiece? What if it requires that people look at the screen more than me?

People who do demos are not exonerated from the principles of effective communication. By definition, a demo is just a form of evidence. It should be in support of something you want them to think, feel and do. Since you are the most important visual aid in the room—or should be—you still need to focus their attention and share your plan and intention for them first, using good eye contact from the front of the room where all can see you. You have then earned the right to tell them where to look and when—even if you do have to become a disembodied voice from the back of the room for a period of time. It doesn't hurt to occasionally walk up and point to what you want them to see—it'll be all the more effective because you are taking the time to deliberately do it. And, don't forget, you can reclaim the front of the room when you conclude and articulate what you want them to think, feel and do as a result of what they've just heard and seen.

What about gestures and filler words? People tell me I have too many/too few gestures and repeat words. How can I correct these issues?

I haven't said much about these until now, because they tend to become a non-issue with my approach. Generally, if my clients are focused enough on their audience strategy, have a map for the flow of their key messages, and have run through it a few times—the gestures often work organically and the filler words are minimized and conversational. They look and sound ready, authentic and engaged with the audience. Gestures may need tweaking at the very most (usually it's about how big and how often, which should mirror the general type/frequency used by your decision-makers in the room based on their communication style). However, getting overly focused on controlling your hands or avoiding fillers can be a performance distraction. It's easier to focus on what you should be doing, rather than getting caught up in trying hard to avoid something.

When it comes to gestures, *you should be using them for the benefit of your audience.* Like movement, gestures make you a visual aid. That means things like nervous twitching and repetitive movement tend to go away when you can slow down, anticipate your thoughts and get physically in sync with them.

It's simply a matter of re-directing the nervous energy into something more constructive for the audience:

▶ directing the focus of the audience to a particular place on a slide
▶ describing something visually with your hands
▶ conveying an emotion with your face
▶ enumerating your points or
▶ underscoring words with a deliberate hand signal, etc.

Likewise, fillers are minimized as a result of using the four-step process to get out of your head and get more focused on relating to your audience. Most people use fillers either because they don't know what they are going to say next or are afraid of the silent pause. Focusing instead on things like the flow of your map and eye contact, and using the space created by pausing for purposeful things like gesture, modulation, and emphasis obviate the nervous need for fillers. (See **Step Four: The How**)

Gestural and filler issues are habits. They indicate a lack of consciousness and presence. When you replace them

> *Gestural and filler issues are habits. They indicate a lack of consciousness and presence. When you replace them with purposeful techniques, they tend to die a natural death for most people.*

with purposeful techniques, they tend to die a natural death for most people.

What if rules dictate that you must use a podium or present while seated on stage?

There are times when it's just not politically correct to do the things that would actually be best for the audience. In these cases, you must consider your relationship with the audience as primary and see these situations as opportunities to gently introduce them to a better way. Here are two examples.

I once worked with an executive who was presenting to the U.S. Postmaster General and his team of leaders who sat at an enormous round table. The executive said leaving the podium just wasn't done—even though the postmaster and half his team were seated in big leather chairs with their backs to him, necessitating that they view his presentation on monitors mounted in the corners of the room opposite the podium.

Odd as it was, the solution was to stay at the podium as required, but use animation (i.e., gestures that could be seen above the podium and the occasional step to the side of the podium for emphasis) and very deliberate eye contact directed to the back of most people's heads. The goal was to create an effect that was so very real, personal and engaging on the screen that the listeners would be compelled to turn around and engage with the speaker—which is exactly what they did. This was my client's measure of success.

Another client of mine prepared a ten-minute presentation as requested by the organizer of an industry conference, after which she was told she would sit down and participate in a panel discussion with four other presenters who had done the same. No other guidance was provided until two days before the event when I got a frantic call from my client. She had just learned that the organizer and other presenters—who clearly hadn't yet prepared their respective remarks—decided that they would huddle on a couch up on the huge stage and casually banter about industry trends and their implications while the audience looked on.

My client was disheartened because she had spent time preparing a researched point of view and motivational message for the association membership and saw this as an opportunity to position her company as an industry leader. She figured that all her time had been wasted and that she had no other option than to play by the new rules.

As I saw it, the situation had all the marks of a group of people who were a) avoiding their responsibilities as guest speakers; and b) trying to make themselves feel safer by resorting to the lowest common denominator—sitting up there and winging it for ninety minutes. My other observation was that the organizer/moderator probably didn't know how to structure the interaction in a way that would provide the audience with any real value. This presented an opportunity for my client: there was a void, and she already had what was needed to fill it.

This wasn't immediately apparent to my client, who was concerned that she would appear overly confident and show-up the other presenters. I told her that this might be an unintended consequence, but that she needed to get clear about her real audience—the membership. Besides, her thematic approach, heartfelt words and professional delivery would make the moderator realize that inviting her was the smartest decision he ever made.

In the end, she presented as we had rehearsed with the slight adjustment of beginning her opening from a seated position. As she got more animated and into her point, it seemed natural for her to ask that one key slide be shown and request a microphone so she could point something out (arrangements for which she made ahead of time with the moderator's permission). When finished, she walked to the edge of the stage to bring her message to the audience. She later reported that it was as though the event suddenly came alive. Her inspirational tag line caught fire and everyone—the moderator, audience members asking questions, and even the other presenters—kept referring to it and her insights as they built on her point of view. The program was a success for everyone—but especially for my client who had stepped up to add real value.

> *Connect with your audience first in a way they expect. Then you've earned the right to (subtly) ask them to tolerate something a bit different . . .*

So, connect with your audience first in a way they expect. Then you've earned the right to (subtly) ask them to tolerate something a bit different in the interest of giving them the most satisfying and productive outcome possible.

What if I can't see many audience members from the stage?

Sometimes stage lighting is such that audience members in the third row and beyond are nothing but shadowy figures. Nevertheless, you still have to work the room with eye contact if you are going to make it feel like an intimate conversation and less of a performance.

First, don't overlook the fact that lighting can be adjusted. Production folks are notorious for blasting the stage with light for consistent effect, but have a control panel of options available to them for making the lighting just right for each and every speaker or event on the stage. You just have to ask them—and most are delighted to problem solve with you.

Beyond that, be intrepid about targeting your eye contact in these large forums—even if it means delivering one-unit-of-thought per ghost or per table. Also, don't forget the individuals in those front rows who paid more to see you (ahem). Performers tend to look past them to avoid the possible tension or discomfort, when more personal eye contact with those seated upfront actually makes a presenter appear more comfortable and approachable—especially to the back row watching you on the big screen. (Refer to the discussion on eye contact in **Step Four: The How**).

What is the correct way to work with visual aids?

Since you are indeed the most important visual aid in the room, I have left a discussion of the use of slides, flip charts, white boards, and handouts as the last consideration—even though most presenters think it's the most pressing consideration. If you develop your story or business case first, the visuals are the easy part and should consume less of your time.

As noted earlier in **Step Three: The Way,** visual aids should only be used to serve your audience by 1) providing supportive evidence for your key messages in the form of pictures, graphs, steps or data; and/or 2) visually reinforcing *the essence of* your most important key messages with select words or phrases (not sentences and paragraphs). They should not be your scripted remarks.

I have also discussed how movement to and from your visual aids (see **Step Four: The How**) should be your way of telling the audience where to look and when.

Controlling the focus of the audience is really at the core of effectively creating and using any type of visual aid. As such, it is simply an extension of your use of eye contact.

For this reason, I strongly discourage you from referencing slides on your own computer monitor (rather than using the same screen the audience is viewing) with the reasoning that it keeps you facing the audience. This actually makes things harder for the audience by leaving them on their own to navigate your slides. You should be helping the audience

> *Controlling the focus of the audience is really at the core of effectively creating and using any type of visual aid. As such, it is simply an extension of your use of eye contact.*

navigate your slides like a leader instead of marginalizing your-self in the corner with your computer or occasionally flashing a laser pointer from the sidelines.

There is a three-step choreography for more effectively in-teracting with visual aids (including slides, flip charts, white boards, etc.) that is taught by many coaches, including myself. Once mastered, it has implications for how you create visual aids as well. It is called *touch, turn, talk:*

1. *Touch the visual aid physically or with your eyes* to direct the focus of the audience to a specific point on your slide or chart. (Touching includes writing on a flip chart.) Do this during a silent pause and use this time to take in the information yourself to make sure what they see and what you are about to say actually match. This means no sweeping gestures or glances in the general direction of a slide.

2. *Turn away from the visual aid and reengage with the au-dience.* This is critical, since you want to maintain the connection with the audience that you've worked so hard to establish from the beginning of your presentation. By doing so, you are telling your audience to also disengage from the visual aid and look back to you for an explana-tion of what they've just seen.

3. *Begin talking, using the one-unit-of-thought-to-one-person eye contact technique* **(see Step Four: The How).** This is the home base to which you must always return, as

opposed to getting lost—along with your audience—in the details of your visual aid.

This technique is a bit of a coordination exercise and often requires that someone watch you in rehearsal to see if you are actually doing it correctly. Surprisingly, it does not have to appear as robotic as it sounds. Once mastered, it simply keeps you oriented toward the audience and inserts helpful pauses that allow you to spoon-feed your audience complex information in digestible bites. (*Now we look at this together, and now you look at me while I talk. Now we look here again...*)

While you are perfecting this technique, make sure you at least keep the overall goal of showing the audience where to look and when in mind. Observe these basics:

▶ If you have slides, please reference them. They are not wallpaper. There is nothing more challenging for a listener than having to ping-pong back and forth between you and a visual aid to make sense of things.

▶ If you hear yourself saying things like "as you can see" or in any way referencing or looking at the slide, get yourself over to it and show them *specifically* where to look.

▶ When you catch yourself spending more time with your slide than the audience—stop. Consciously return to your eye contact technique.

In conclusion, here are a few other small steps you can take for big impact when it comes to keeping the audience with you.

▶ Don't show the audience anything you don't want them to see at that moment. If you do, it becomes an immediate distraction. Here are ways to ensure you control their focus:

  ■ Don't distribute handouts or show agenda slides before your opening remarks. If you talk over these, be prepared to repeat yourself later, because they will not have heard you.

  ■ Don't put multiple charts on the same slide for the sake of only having one slide. Sequence the visual information to make it easier to follow.

  ■ Verbally set up the next complex chart or graph with introductory information the audience may need *before* revealing it.

  ■ Build complex slides, revealing one component or bullet point at a time. Use this technique sparingly, since it can be experienced as overly controlling by an audience.

  ■ Use short phrases rather than full sentences in bulleted slides to make it easier for you to guide your audience's focus.

▶ Use the letter "B" Key (a function that blanks out the screen, available in PowerPoint slide show mode only) or the blank screen button on your remote for an effective—and dramatic—way to gain the focus of your audience. Starting front and center with a blank screen behind you throughout your Opening, or shutting down before beginning your Conclusion, are purposeful places to insert this technique.

▶ Consider using more than one type of visual aid. Would telling the story be easier and more engaging than showing another case study slide? How about working through the equation on a white board instead? What about stopping and handing out that busy chart so they can better see it and ask questions? Or would it be easier on the audience to make your point by just showing the two most important figures on the chart instead of showing the whole chart?

> *Consider using more than one type of visual aid. Would telling the story be easier and more engaging than showing another case study slide?*

Whatever you do, get their attention first, direct their focus, and then tell them what you want them to know. And please do make sure that what they are supposed to see is visible and readable from all points in the room.

While I hope you have gleaned a few tips from reading through these FAQs, I also hope you have had a BFO (Blinding Flash of the Obvious) experience. That's as it should be when you are audience-focused and know why you are doing what you're doing. Then, even if the situation doesn't go as planned or the room isn't configured perfectly, you can still make a strategic call and deliver an extraordinarily good experience for your audience.

TAKING THE MEASURE
OF YOUR SUCCESS

*Optional, but highly
recommended*

P RESENTING IS A means to an end, a so-called *soft
skill* that gets really hard if we don't practice it in various
situations. For this reason, I'm often asked about recommen-
dations for continued improvement.

REVIEW THE FOUR STEPS AS
PART OF YOUR DEBRIEF

My first recommendation is to use the four-step process as
an evaluative tool *after* delivering a presentation. Do a postmor-
tem assessment of your presentation or meeting to determine
what you may have missed in reading your audience, or to what

extent you may have overreached in setting your objective, or how things could otherwise have been conveyed. It will set the stage for better outcomes in the future.

But don't forget to pat yourself on the back too. You can't control everything. You can only

> *The measure of your success has to do with how appropriate your ... objective ... was in the first place and how close you actually came to achieving it.*

do a better job of influencing and making the most of every opportunity. The measure of your success has to do with how appropriate your think-feel-do objective for that presentation or interaction was in the first place and how close you actually came to achieving it.

TAKE RISKS AND SEEK OUT INFORMED FEEDBACK

Beyond this, continued improvement becomes a matter of two things: taking new risks and being open to feedback.

A new project or role can come with an abundance of opportunities to take on different audiences and communication challenges. In the absence of these new situations, the next best thing is to proactively create such opportunities at work and after-hours. Joining a group like Toastmasters International*

---

* See www.toastmasters.org

is fine—as long as you can filter the feedback offered through what you've learned here. (Non-professional organizations can sometimes be a situation of the blind leading the blind when it comes to strategies and techniques.)

Sometimes, watching a single video recording of something you've done can feel like a big risk and more than enough feedback, thank you very much. But as your high-stakes audiences change throughout your career, I urge you to seek out and take advantage of training and coaching from people like me offered by your business or professional organization. That way you can keep your skills sharp and get a more balanced assessment.

But nothing can replace getting constructive feedback from an informed audience member who was in the room with you. I invite you to share this book with your co-presenters and teams, so that you all learn the same approach and vocabulary around presentation. The advantage is that effectiveness with the audience will always be your lodestar or strategic guide, versus "this worked for me once" or "you should never do that." In fact, when I train a team that works together regularly, a corollary teambuilding benefit is precisely this built-in mechanism for continued improvement. In business, we rarely get more than a "hey, nice presentation" comment after a meeting. But an informed mentor or teammate who was there can help you honestly track your development.

ENJOY THE SENSE OF MASTERY

The focus of this book has been about how to work the process. Perhaps not enough has been said about the satisfaction and ease that come purely from gaining increased mastery and professionalism along the way. It manifests as a little voice that advises and encourages you as you move through a presentation or meeting.

It says things like, *I've seen this before, and I can handle this*; or *That's interesting, this is not getting the response I expected*; or *I better pause and ask a question to find out what's going on*; or *Good question, I'll remember that for next time*, or *They're with me now, this is going nicely*. It sounds quite different from the distracting fears that used to run through your head. Instead, you are actually present and have Presence.

It's not a permanent state, however; it has to be conjured again and again. That means—just when you think you've seen and done it all—you must listen to and ask questions about your audience until you discover what's unique about them and go through the process yet again.

This energy and dedication is ultimately what separates the extraordinary business communicator from the ordinary. It's called curiosity—about other people, their ideas, emotional needs and unique situations. It's what has kept training and coaching this methodology fresh for me for over a decade.

Stay curious, my friends!

ABOUT THE AUTHOR

Kate LeVan trains, coaches and collaborates on business communication effectiveness with major corporations worldwide and as an instructor at Northwestern University's Kellogg School of Management. Her training consistently receives top ratings from executive development program participants for its simplicity, applicability and career-changing impact.

Kate's career in advertising and marketing allowed her to observe the edge that effective communication gives business professionals across all industries. Her company, LeVan Partners, LLC is dedicated to helping clients build strong business relationships through greater clarity, authenticity, empathy and impact in their face-to-face and virtual communication.

Kate commutes to O'Hare International Airport and beyond from Evanston, Illinois, where she resides with her husband. For information on how you or your team can experience Kate's training firsthand, go to *LeVanPartners.com* or *SpeakingwithStrategicImpact.com*.

CPSIA information can be obtained
at www.ICGtesting.com
Printed in the USA
FFOW05n1234190617
36802FF